SKI

MEMOIRS OF A VIETNAM VET

Revised Edition

SKI

MEMOIRS OF A VIETNAM VET

Revised Edition

AL SUTTON

ANOINTED LIFE PUBLISHING COMPANY
Phoenix, Arizona

SKI
By Al Sutton

© Copyright 2012 by Al Sutton.

All rights reserved. No portion of this book may be reproduced, stored in a retrieval system or transmitted in any form electronic, mechanical, photocopy, recording or any other except for brief quotations in printed reviews, without prior consent of the publisher.

Printed in the United States of America

Library of Congress Control Number: 2011960161

ISBN: 978-0-692-25239-0

Editing by Keith H. Chambers

Cover Design by C W Technology Consulting

www.anointedlifepublishing.com

Dedication

To my wife, Sarah; I thank God for you and truly believe that your love and understanding of my condition (PTSD) is why I am still alive and writing this story, instead of acting it out.

Also, to the men and women of the armed forces who put themselves in harm's way to defend our great country.

Contents

Dedication..v

Preface..viii

Acknowledgements..xi

Chapter 1 Option X..1

Chapter 2 Can't Miss...17

Chapter 3 Show Time..29

Chapter 4 The Marine 33

Chapter 5 Insanity 49

Chapter 6 Destiny 57

Chapter 7 Rehab 73

Chapter 8 Autobiography of a Nobody..79

Chapter 9 News 87

Chapter 10 The Wall...93

Appendix A The Nut Ward...105

NOT EVERYONE

WHO LOST HIS LIFE IN VIETNAM

DIED THERE.

NOT EVERYONE

WHO CAME HOME FROM VIETNAM

EVER LEFT THERE

Preface

I joined the Marine Corps in 1966 and in December of that same year, was sent to Vietnam. As a UH-1E helicopter gunship crew chief, I served two (2) thirteen month tours of duty and was awarded: Combat Aircrew Wings w/3 stars, the Presidential Unit Citation, nineteen (19) Combat Air Medals (including Air Medal with Bronze Star), the Vietnam Campaign Medal w/device, the Vietnam Service Medal w/1 star, the National Defense Ribbon, and Good Conduct Medal. At the end of my second tour, I was given an early out from the corp.

I then attended and graduated from Los Angeles Trade Technical College with an A.S. degree in Aviation Technology. Employed as an aircraft mechanic, I worked for several aviation companies including: Bell Helicopters, Douglas Aircraft, and Evergreen Airlines.

It was in 1989 that I first began to suffer from what I would later learn was Post-Traumatic Stress Disorder (PTSD) and in February of that year I found myself on a psychiatric ward at the Westwood VA Hospital. Later, I was assigned to out-patient status where a counselor suggested that I write poems or short stories to help relieve some of the stress that I was experiencing.

In December of 1996, I returned to the VA psychiatric ward and remained there until October of 1997. I included brief excerpts of my notes from that stay in this book—to give the reader some understanding of what that experience was like.

From the beginning, I did not write "Ski" with the idea that it would become a book. Rather, it evolved from that collection of poems and short stories that provided a sort of therapy for me while I was on the psychiatric ward. That collection was originally intended to be my last will and testament as I contemplated doing horrific acts that would no doubt lead to my death.

It was only by the grace of God and the remembrance of the good marines that I had met along the way that saved me. Instead of a "suicide by police," I focused my energies in a more positive way. That is how "Ski," with its message of hope and rebirth became a reality.

I sincerely hope that the reader gains a better appreciation of the sacrifices that veterans have made in the service of our country; and that those who continue to suffer gain the help and the respect that they deserve.

Acknowledgements

Congresswoman Maxine Waters—without your help, the Vietnam Veterans of America, Chapter 713 would not have been possible.

Doctor Grieder—thanks for your understanding of the mental pain I was in; you always had time.

Marty Moore, congressional aid—there are no words to describe the love and respect I have for you. You were the rope that held me up.

Candace, Torrance VA Center, PTSD group leader—thank you for the coping skills you taught us and for the special hug you gave to those vets who were having a really bad day.

Bullet Bob Sheppard, vice president of Vietnam Veterans of America, Chapter 713—God sent you to me at the lowest point of my life; because of you I have Christ in my life. May you rest in peace.

Karen Burman, Inglewood Veterans Center—thanks for advising me to write poems and/or notes as a way to help me deal with PTSD. It was the best advice anyone ever gave to me.

My PTSD group brothers at the Gardena Vet Center. Thank you so much.

My PTSD group brothers at Lancaster Community Clinic, 547 W. Lancaster Blvd. Though we passed as strangers in the night, I will never forget your kindness.

My present PTSD group (Phoenix Vet Center). Without your help, I would have ended up in my garage with the door closed and the car motor running. Every Monday that we meet, I am reminded that because you can, I can. Thanks.

Chapter 1

Option X

In the darkened room, the years after Vietnam played themselves over and over on the big screen in Ralph's mind. "Who gives a damn?" he muttered. He then laughed at how he'd been talking to himself a lot lately. He remembered his mother once telling him that it was okay to talk to yourself as long as you didn't answer. He wondered if he was now answering himself. After thinking about it for a few seconds, Ralph decided that it was unimportant. Besides, being crazy could only help his situation, and he would need all of the help he could get for what he planned to do. For Ralph, it was time to get even.

He sat in the small room alone and stared out the window. Outside of his apartment was his own personal Vietnam. In fact, it was worse than Vietnam. In Nam, all you had to do was stay alive—with the hope of going home and getting away from the human slaughter. Outside of this window, the world dictated terms for living; not death. This was normal, at least for everyone else, but not for him. For the people here, their war was family, love, religion, home, work, school, bills, responsibility, and even respect for human life, but it wasn't his. He had taken all of those things for granted and now they were no longer important.

Yes, he had managed to stay alive in Nam, but that had come at a price. And if one thirteen month tour messed up a man's head and could change his values, Ralph wondered what his two tours had done to his head. He thought of those poor souls who volunteered to join the

Army after 9/11. They were the soldiers who went to Iraq and Afghanistan for four and even five tours of duty. He couldn't even imagine how messed up their heads were. He guessed that it was like doing twenty years the hard way.

At least in Nam, because of the draft, a soldier could do time, get out, and then be replaced by new meat for the grinder. Without a draft however, America could care less about these new era soldiers—whether they lived, died, or lost their minds. A nice parade, a pat on the back, and then they would be forgotten; compliments of Bush, his boss Dick Cheney, and his boys at Halliburton government contracts. Follow the money baby—just follow the money—not the body bags. It was crap like this, still going on right now, that kept a sour taste in his mouth. Anyway, nothing he could do about it now. *God help our troops.*

It had been nearly forty years and Ralph was still trying to figure out Vietnam and his part in it. *Yea, that's the problem all right.* He had never left Nam. He remembered gun runs, firefights, and dead people; lots and lots of dead people. His life was just a firefight. Even today his days were numbered, his friends were limited, and his jobs were unimportant.

And then there was love. He wondered how one falls in love when your days and nights are spent searching your mind; going over and over in your head what the war had really been about. In Vietnam, who, what, and why were important—everything else was bull. There, he had learned not to look to the future. There was no future, no past, just Nam. The years since had gone so quickly that he still couldn't quite believe it was nearly 2010.

He was stuck in the past. While the people below his fifth-story window talked love, business, the future, and all that happy stuff, he was reliving the deaths of friends, the fear and terror of a firefight, and the burning helicopters, filled with troops, plunging to the ground and exploding into a million pieces. He remembered the sticky mud of the jungle, the booby traps, the ambushes, the crying of the wounded, and the wax-like surprised look on the faces of the dead. That was his world. No one had debriefed him when he returned to civilian life, and it had proven impossible to live in this world and Nam at the same time.

And so it would be from the window that he was staring out of, that the final drama of his life would unfold. He had failed to survive in their world, but now he would relieve the pain of his world. People would know that from this day forward, he had lived and served in a world tougher than any; one that only a combat veteran could understand and survive. Once they knew, they would be sorry for the disrespect, sorry for not debriefing him, and sorry that they did not try to understand what he had been going through for these however many years.

This would be his personal 9/11—a final good-bye to his country. Yes, the same country that had used him and then tossed him aside. He was home now, but so was his personal war; as real as ever. He thought of a poem he had written and how it summed up his present condition. He started to say it to himself.

Al Sutton

A.S.N

Another Sleepless Night

Another sleepless night
Damn here I go again
I think maybe I'm dead already
And every night my eternity in hell

If only I had died in combat
Saluted by my fellow marines
They would mourn for only a moment
Knowing death is part of being a marine

At midnight the graveyards open
And the march of the K.I.A.s begin
I salute them as they pass
While feeling his own survival had to be a sin

I comfort myself with how very blessed I am since Nam
I've lived so many years
Still before the night is over
I will have cried a million tears

In my pain long before daylight
I'll think of calling out to my veteran friends
But instead I'll pray my comrades
Are having better nights

And I would rather fall on my sword
Than draw them into my hellish fight
If only there was somewhere to run
Or better yet, an enemy to fight

Fix bayonets and attack
Anything, any desperate thing
But please, Lord please
Not another long, long night

After saying the poem, he started to laugh aloud, but instantly thought of the stupid looks on the faces of people he would kill and the fear on the faces of the ones he was going to kill. For reasons that he couldn't explain, he found himself fighting back tears that had somehow found their way to angry eyes. But, he refused the tears permission to run. He was going to do this and that was all there was to it! *WHOO-RAH MOTHER SUCKERS!*

Chill bumps raced over Ralph's body. He knew it was fear, but fear was not an unfamiliar feeling. In Nam, he faced real fear too many times; it was just something you had to overcome. He'd felt that nervous sour stomach and heart pounding fear, on each of the countless times his helicopter came under enemy fire. He felt it when an operation went bad and some young, scared, radio-man called for air support and Medevac, as "Charlie" threatened to overrun their position. Fear and a constant rattle of gunfire went hand in hand. He could still hear the enemy's AK-47s and the panicked voices of his fellow Marines on the radios. Suddenly, his fear brought back memories that seemed all too real.

"Hostage 2-0, we're taking fire! We're taking fire in the zone!" The call on the radio was from the pilot of a twin-bladed, CH-46 rescue helicopter (call sign Seaworthy) as it attempted to load wounded marines in a designated LZ (landing zone). He desperately needed help from Ralph's gunship helicopter (call sign Hostage 2-0) and its four man crew.

Immediately, Ralph's pilot put the gunship on course while the co-pilot armed the ship's guns and rockets. Ralph and his door gunner also prepared for battle by stacking several hundred rounds of belted M-60 ammunition for rapid reloading of their M-60 machine guns. Everyone tried to locate the direction of the enemy fire below, being directed at Seaworthy. After spotting the tree line where the bad guys were shooting from, Ralph's helicopter prepared to return fire in that direction. Within seconds, the gunship dove to earth with its four exterior machine guns blazing.

The helicopter developed "G" forces on the way down that forced Ralph to hold tightly onto the machine gun mount. When they were in range, he fired several bursts from the M-60 into the tree line, where he saw muzzle flashes, even before he heard the sound of North Vietnamese gunfire. "You're taking fire!" A grunt radio man on the ground screamed at them through his mike; warning them of what they already knew. The enemy had switched targets and was now concentrating most of his gunfire at Ralph's helicopter.

As Hostage 2-0 continued to dive toward the earth, the pilot switched from guns to rockets, but could only fire four before he had to climb out of the gun run, banking sharply in an attempt to avoid fire from the enemy. Ralph and the door gunner, now the only defense, poured M-60 fire into the tree line, as they climbed and banked away from danger.

There was a sudden noise on the radio again. "Hostage 2-O, this is Seaworthy. We're coming out; we're coming out westbound!" Seaworthy was leaving the landing zone. "Damn It!" Ralph's pilot, Major Swift's yell was so loud that he could be heard above the shooting, the jet engine, and the flapping noise of the helicopter blades.

6

Option X

"We're out of position to cover you Seaworthy. You copy?" Swift's voice sounded desperate, "You copy?" Despite the huge amount of gunfire, Seaworthy's pilot answered, in a very calm voice, "Yea, I copy Hostage 2-0. We're out of here, westbound—westbound—I need gun cover. We're still taking hits."

Swift banked sharply back into the direction of the tree line in an attempt to put the gunship back into position to cover Seaworthy. Ralph continued to cover Seaworthy's departure with his single machine gun; any return fire was better than none; otherwise Seaworthy was doomed. In fact, for a second or two, it looked as if that was the case anyway. Ralph watched as pieces of the rescue helicopter were blown off by enemy machine gun fire; at least some of which seemed to be heavy 51-caliber weapons. Even if those weapons were not radar controlled, they were equivalent to helicopter gunfire.

"I'm in hot!" Swift yelled, as he again attempted to line up the helicopter with the tree line. Suddenly, Ralph realized that they were only about fifteen hundred feet above the ground. There was only enough time for just a few seconds of shooting; and then they would have to pull up or risk slamming into the ground.

Suddenly, as Swift shot rockets into the tree line, there was a series of six explosions—all in a neat little row. Most of the gunfire then stopped. At that same moment, Seaworthy was able to bank away and start a fast climb. They were safe.

For Ralph and his crew, pounding hearts and flushed faces were the only reminders of another encounter with death. Just like that, it was over as the two helicopters rushed upward into the safety of the Vietnamese sky.

Slightly dazed, Ralph pushed the brief contact with "Charlie" out of his mind. It was history now, and in Nam history didn't count; there were no yesterdays and no tomorrows.

He thought of smoking a joint, but for some reason decided not to. After all, sitting here with weapons and waiting for the sun to announce that it was time to start killing folks, had him higher than a stick of weed could ever get him. The weed could wait. Instead, his mind turned to one of the few things that had given him a chance to put things in perspective: his poetry.

For years, on the recommendations of his first Veterans Administration shrink, Ralph wrote hundreds of poems based on his thoughts about Nam and a veteran's life after combat. He thought of his group brothers: fellow Vietnam vets. As messed up as he was, most of them had been meeting every Monday morning between ten-thirty and twelve noon for over three decades at the Veterans Center in Torrance, California. It was there, after years of meeting with his sick vet buddies and listening to doctors, shrinks, and non-combat college grads, that he wrote the poem, "Group." It seemed to sum up all that he and the vets had learned. He tried to recall it, but except for war experiences, his memory had been a problem since Nam. It was kind of like he didn't want to remember. Anyway, that's why he wrote them down.

Feeling stupid, Ralph reached for the M-60 ammo can where he stored his poems along with a short story that he hoped would put some money in his two daughter's pockets, after he finished doing what he had to do. He wanted to be sure that, through his story, they would know his reasons for the killings. He could only pray that his death was worth more than his life had been since the war. After looking through about twenty poems he found it and began to read out loud. As always, he found comfort reading his poems.

Group

We recite a prayer of helplessness
And our search for answers begins
Aging warriors guided by so called professionals
Back thru a war that never ends

Men confused and seeking solutions
Each believing himself the blame
A dozen of America's finest
Their stories all the same

My best friend died at Khe Sanh
The lieutenant got his legs blown off
Brother Moe was killed in Operation Hasting II
In Hobo Woods first platoon was lost

Post-Traumatic Stress
The human price of a killing field
Depression; a veteran's down payment
Intrusive thoughts of their G.I. Bill

Memories, memories, and nightmares
Cold sweats and silent pain
Life in the twenty-first century
For these survivors of Vietnam

Attempts to treat what's incurable
A game they'll never win
While group relieves their itching
The cancer of war continues to eat

Al Sutton

Shrinks, pills, and nut wards
Prescriptions for a dying mind
It will work, doctors say, if you work it
People paid for wasting our time

My name is veteran nobody
And I suffer from PTSD
Today I'm feeling hurt and rage
Life has lost its meaning to me

Homicide and suicide
Are the subjects avoided the most
But alone in the dark of morning, unlike group
Each is always close

Enemy tracers, dying screams
Total madness, booby traps, snakes, and bugs
America's forgotten remembers
While trying to convert hate to love

    After reading the poem, Ralph felt a little better about what he was about to do. He even smiled, as he thought about what his group brothers would say on the first Monday that they meet after learning what one of their own had done. He was sure most of them also wanted to do the same. He could imagine the headline in the Los Angeles Times that would also include a picture of him taken from the M-60 ammo can. The headlines would read: Homeless Vietnam vet kills twenty before he's killed by police! The accompanying picture would reveal him to be not very different from a lot of black brothers in Central Los Angeles: six feet tall and about one hundred and forty pounds, with light brown skin, thick wavy hair, and brown eyes. *To find out more, they'll have to read my work.*

He thought of his weed again, then reached into his pants pocket and pulled out a joint. *Might as well*, he thought, *it's stupid to waste good weed.* He lit up and began drifting back to Vietnam, but the persistent blaring of a car horn caused his mind to return. Recovering, he found it amazing that after all of these many years, he could still recall the war with such clarity and yet, after each memory had come, there was a feeling that something was missing. There was always a lost memory on the tip of his mental tongue. He had come to believe that if only he could understand this feeling, remember what it was, or if it was anything at all, that he might solve the puzzle. Try as he might, no answers came.

The tears came again. This time, he tried but couldn't will them back. *It's just life.* He reached for the comfort of the M-1 carbine leaning against the wall next to him. *In reality it wasn't Nam that had caused me all my problems, it was coming back home; back to a country run by dumb asses.* Ralph checked the safety on the carbine and then examined the weapon with expert eyes. *No more problems, no more messed-up jobs, and no more silly—non-understanding—selfish wives.* Yes, all his problems would soon be over, and if things work the way he planned, Crystal and Amber, his two daughters by his second wife, would be provided for, by a grateful press. He knew that Alicia, his daughter by his first wife, was doing okay. Her aunt had left her a little something and besides that, she was an agent for the feds.

His mind drifted back to what the headlines would say and how the very people who would sensationalize what he was about to do, would play into his hands.

Ralph believed that the news media would love a story of so many innocent killings without (as far as they are concerned) any rational reason. All that they would have to go on was what he was leaving behind for them: his story. The title had been chosen carefully: "Option X: The Ending." It was a catchy title that was about to be finalized from the window that he was sitting next to now. His many poems would also help to tell the story of war and its effect on the lives of the people that fight wars for no purpose other than to profit big business—there was no better example than Dick Cheney and his very own Halliburton. The story had to be told and with the giving of his life, it would be.

He sucked in another deep drag. *Man this is good weed.* Smiling, he held the joint up for inspection, before putting it out and sliding the remainder into his pocket. *It really is good; proper for my upcoming ten minutes of fame.* He prayed for a quick death. Pain was something he was not good at. He then pulled a handful of poems from the M-60 ammo can to console himself and fingered through them quickly until two short ones caught his attention.

Writing poems had saved his life until now and so it was only right that his creations should play a part in his death. He read the first short poem. It seemed to sum up, in a few lines, one of his constant dreams. The other poem was a dream that was about to come true.

Option X

Ambush

Without warning suddenly
Soldiers were scrambling under heavy enemy fire
Seems like only enemy tracers flying
Ambush, we're going to die

Our units fighting bravely
I try, but something's wrong
And then the jungle disappears
Ambush—but I'm at home

Al Sutton

Poison

I could really face life better
Living like I've already died
If hidden inside my hollow tooth
A capsule of cyanide

What a power it would be
Knowing death is but a bite away
My enemies never to see me suffer
I die whenever I say

Maybe I'll just go crazy
And kill everyone in sight
Then deprive the survivors of justice
By taking a single bite

Thoughts of Viet-Nam
And those little rats-like things, rushing into the sea
Bless all who are about to die
What must be, will be!

What a trip. If he really had a capsule of cyanide, it would really piss everybody off. He could be dead before a single police bullet could touch him—no police hero. Talk about depriving the people, which he hated, of justice. He laughed out loud. *Wow, just one little cyanide capsule; a single bite and there would be no hero to get credit for killing me.*

Maybe he might kill 30 or even more of his non-caring fellow Americans, who did not hesitate to send soldiers and his fellow marines to fight their wars for profit. Today, it would be their mothers, their fathers, their sisters, their brothers, and their uncles who would be killed for nothing, just as his fellow marines had died for nothing— nothing but corporate profits.

After today, many shocked families would suffer from PTSD, just like him. Maybe then, like the survivors of 9/11, or those who lost loved ones that day, they would understand that wars, for those who fight them, never end. And since he had no death pill, he would, if they didn't get him first, blow his own brains out. Ralph knew how upset it made his countrymen when a killer takes his own life. He started laughing and couldn't stop. He laughed until his side started to hurt. No hero to make them feel better. "That's a good one," he said out loud. He held his hurting side and continued laughing.

Chapter 2

Can't Miss

While the time was approaching and the darkness outside was starting to fade, Ralph wondered again how many people he would kill before they took him out. Not that it really mattered—just as long as it was more than that marine had killed at that college in Texas in the 1960's. From this day forward, America would know that he'd lived his life as a warrior and no longer just a forgotten veteran. Yes, they would remember him now; moreover, they would also want to understand him because today, a lot of them were going to be dead. And he, well he would die like a marine with some honor. He would be a soldier again. Just like his friend Joe C. once said, "All soldiers go to heaven." Somehow that seemed funny to Ralph and he laughed aloud again. *Not this time killer*, he said to himself. *Not this time.*

Sunlight began finding its way through small holes in the apartment's yellowed window shade, and Ralph was able to see the cheap table next to the single, worn out, bed more clearly. It was hard to believe what his life had become. Instead of owning property and cars and having enough money to do pretty much as he pleased, it had come to this. He'd worked his way out of the ghetto, but a few bad breaks and a few wives later, he now had nothing. To make matters worse, Nam was back.

Shaking his head in disgust, he made a clicking sound with his tongue. "Poor thing," he said aloud. "Poor little thing! There's nobody to help poor Ralph." He laughed aloud at his own sarcastic humor. *Better to laugh than to cry.* And laughing out loud relieved his stress. He sat on the edge of the bed and looked out at the sunlight, bright against the window shade. In another hour the downtown streets of Los Angeles, below his window, would be full of people and traffic.

The downtown masses were people from all over. They were people of different cultures, people of different colors, and people of different classes who come to shop and work in what Ralph considered to be neutral territory. Downtown was a place where the rich, the famous, the proud, and the poor gather to stare at one another—all agreeing they are the better for their experience. *Today will be an exception.*

Some of you fools are going to die today just like we did over there in Nam, without any warning. BLAM! You're dead. BLAM! Another hit. BLAM! Another one falls. BLAM! People falling like flies: ten, twelve, sixteen, and the police have not even arrived. BLAM! Now there's nineteen. BLAM! Twenty souls, hopefully more, will pay for veterans everywhere.

Ralph walked the short distance to the window and lifted the shade to look down at the people below preparing for another normal boring day; knowing that for many, it would be their last. A Remington 300 sniper's rifle leaned against the wall near the window. Placing the carbine next to it, he carefully began figuring out his best fields of fire. He moved to the opposite side of the window to observe the more populated area on his right. That was when he noticed a uniformed marine across the street about a half a block downstream. To his amazement, the marine appeared to be staring directly up at him. Instinctively, he backed away from the window and the marine's line of sight.

Ralph had picked this building to rent, specifically because of its location—it was directly in line with Alameda Street which ended at 7th street. He had a field of fire from his window straight down Alameda for nearly three blocks, including the three crossing intersections of 4th, 5th, and 6th street. On both sides of Alameda were the beginnings of dozens of discount stores and restaurants.

To his left, he had a clear field of fire down into the intersection of Central and 7th Street and clear shots into the open windows of the many two and three story buildings just across the street along Alameda.

To his right, there were clear shots into the Spring Street and 7th Street intersection. That particular intersection, Ralph noticed, had at least three seven story buildings that were tall enough for police snipers to be positioned above him. He would be careful to stand back as far as possible when firing in that direction.

He considered the back of his building. Unfortunately, there was an open lot next to the building's rear door. There was nothing he could do about that; it was, in fact, his weak spot and the door to his death. Ralph smiled. It wasn't like he had planned to escape anyway, at least not to this world. *All soldiers go to heaven.*

He was just about to look out the window again to see if the marine was still there when it dawned on him that the marine seemed to have known that he was in the window. He had been looking straight into it. But that was impossible. No one could possibly have known what he planned to do. He brushed it off, figuring that his nerves were getting to him. He returned cautiously to peep out the window again just to be sure it was only his nerves. Not that it would stop anything; he was going to do this anyway.

The marine was gone. Ralph searched the street below in both directions, but there was no marine anywhere. *Maybe he went into a store, because he certainly didn't have time to walk; hell, even run out of my line of sight in the second or two I was away from the window.* Still, in his heart, he knew it was a good thing because, even now, it would be impossible to kill a fellow marine.

That thought, for some reason, made him feel good. "Semper Fi, Jar Head," he said aloud and threw a salute in the direction where he had seen the marine standing. He went on, "Once a marine, always a marine." The core was his family. It was the father he never knew. He could never kill a fellow marine; therefore, any killing would just have to wait until the marine was not in his killing zone. He decided to wait, just in case he had gone into one of the stores that he had been standing in front of. In his mind, a poem that he had written called, "Buddies", recited itself.

Buddies

Today I talked with Private Joe
And Sargent J.J. Hatter
I told them about the nineties
And let them know that they still mattered

They were as I remembered
Very young and full of play
We laughed and cried about the times
We had shared along the way

It felt so good being with them
I asked if I could stay
But they said no
I must be grateful for each and every day

Today I talked with Private Joe and Sargent J.J. Hatter
They died in a place called Vietnam
But to me
That doesn't really matter

For the next twenty minutes Ralph checked and rechecked his weapons. He picked up the loaded magazines and slapped each one hard into his hand to insure that each bullet was properly seated. A jammed weapon would be the last thing he needed, once the shooting started. As the zero hour approached, like a military pass and review, his thoughts turned to his family.

First in line was the old lady, his grandmother. She was a good woman who was strong, loving, and kind; nevertheless, she didn't take any crap from anybody. Until he went to live with her, love was just a word. She was, until her death in 85, always there for him.

On the other hand, there was his mother; who he remembered as young and full of life. She once told him that she had simply gotten pregnant and tried to abort him. He had heard her tell her friends the same story—about trying to get rid of that baby in her stomach. Surprisingly, he understood and never held it against her. Besides, he had his grandmother to take up the slack, and in the process she was both mother and father to him when she took over his life at the age of ten.

He had fared okay, and that was better than he could say about some of his brothers and sisters. But, at least they had lived with their individual fathers for as long as his mother kept them around (sometimes as long as several years). Ralph wished that he had brought alone the poem that he had written about never knowing his own father. It seemed that no one had ever wanted to even talk about it, especially his own mother.

He could hear her answering him now saying, "Boy, I was young, a teenager. Don't keep asking me about who your daddy is—I don't know." After a few years of that garbage, he had stopped asking. Only in his poem did he ever think of his father again. And, what he wrote had surprised him. *Damn.* He wished he had it with him. *Maybe the news media will use it to explain why I killed so many people.* With a little thought, he started to remember the poem and said the title aloud to himself, "Can't Miss". He said it as if he were talking to a room full of college students. *Let's see, how did that poem go?*

Al Sutton

Can't Miss

I never missed my daddy
Can't miss what you never had
But sometimes I dream that he's around
The most wonderful of all the dads

He hugs me all the time
Calls me his little man
He tells me very special things
Only guys can understand

We go to lots of football games
Eat hot dogs, yell, and cheer
Dad showed me how to throw a punch
And explained all men have fear

In my dream if my dad left me
I'd die from being sad
I guess I'm really lucky
Can't miss what you never had

Ralph checked his watch. It was now 07:55. Five minutes left to show time. Leaving the window, he walked the short distance to the room's single bed and placed the ammo can just under it. He stared at it for a few precious seconds. The can contained all that he was. Sitting on the smelly bed's edge, he pulled the ammo can back from underneath the bed and tenderly removed his marine discharge papers. Next, he looked at his medals from Nam, including his prized Single Mission Air Metal with its Bronze Star. His so-called thankful government had mailed it to him instead of presenting it with the ceremony it deserved and required. After all, it had only been his ass on the line. He then removed what was, collectively, the story of his life.

He knew they were a just a bunch of poorly written papers and poems; however, all the important stuff, especially his will, was also included. Any profits from his death, since his grandmother had already passed, would go directly to the only responsibilities he had left on this earth: his three children. He figured that they would get over his death.

The American people would react in a predictable way—that's what Ralph was betting on. They would want to know all there was to know about anyone that had the nerve to quit putting up with the bull and was also willing to kill a bunch of strangers to prove it. He believed that there would be a financial pay-off and that this was the least he could do for his children. No matter what they thought about him, at least they would not be able to say that he didn't try to provide for them.

He thought of his first-born daughter, Alicia, now a government agent; who hated him. He guessed that she blamed him for her mother's death a few years ago. He couldn't figure out why. After all, the ex-wife had deserted Alicia while he was in Iran, where he had worked for over three years back in the 1970's. Fact was, his daughter had actually kept his first wife's death from him. It was only by accident that he found out, over a year after she had been buried. *No matter*. She might still benefit from his final outrage and death.

He loved her. She was still, as he called her, his Little Mama—his first born. He figured that her job had made her a hard ass, but no harder than the marines and Vietnam had hardened him. You could even say, until Beaulah had come into his life, he expected nothing and gave nothing. Yes, Nam had hardened him; to the point that he couldn't help but see all people, even his own children, as dead. That way, should death come, like in the Nam, he would be prepared.

Ralph also thought of the note and poem he was leaving behind to his wonderful and beautiful Beaulah. God, he loved her, and because he loved her, he tried to hate her anyway. After what happened the last time they were together, he had left without a word. Nearly four months had passed since the night he had slipped away. She had done all she could to help him. *Better than those b**ches I married*. He left her a note before leaving. In it, he expressed what he could never say to her face to face; that is, how he felt about her and why he did what he had to do. The note had ended with Ralph asking Beaulah to forgive him. It was hard not to wonder what she would think when she heard the news about him turning the streets of Los Angeles into a killing field.

Thinking about her was starting to make him angry and that was the problem with love. Love causes you to worry about the person that you are in love with. In Nam you saw even your best friends as dead. That way, when they got killed it was okay, because they were dead when you knew them. He reached inside the ammo can and found the poem he had been looking for. As he read it, it seemed silly considering what he was about to do.

Promise

Beaulah, I'm going to love you
No matter what I do
And even though I've left you
I think it's best for you

It's just the times my darling
A lover and a fool
You and me having it all
And me not having a clue

I had hoped I could learn
And grow in your love
While praying my love you would refuse
You promised your love to me

And now that it's all over
You should know
Despite it all
I confess my love for you

Chapter 3

Show Time

Ralph figured that he would be the top gun among the fools that had previously assaulted the public in their own interest—he would kill at least twenty or more civilians before the police arrived. After that, he would concentrate on the police and get as many of them as he could, before they got him. He prayed silently that the police would shoot straight. He didn't want to suffer or somehow be alive when it was all over. A cold sweat appeared on his face as he checked his watch again: two minutes to show time. He began to stack the carbine magazines on the floor near the window. A quick look out the window showed the streets below starting to swell with the city's working class and business types. Cars were already bumper to bumper. He knew that the traffic would be his best barricade to prevent the police from getting too close—too soon.

As he looked out, he noticed a short woman, with a pleasant smile, setting directly across the street on a bus stop bench. She reminded him of his girl, Beaulah. Ralph remembered what it felt like to hold her soft body next to his and the wonderful way they made love together. Beaulah definitely had a way of making him feel special. She was everything that he wanted in a woman: smart and classy with a petite build that was a perfect complement to her soft curly hair and beautiful brown eyes. She was always talking about, "We this, Honey, and "We this, Baby." She was too good for him.

He had tried hard to spare her from his mood swings that occurred mostly on the days when Nam just wouldn't leave him alone. The memories nagged, and sometimes real images would form. Enemy muzzle flashes would appear from freeway tree lines. Even a rain storm would transport him, instantly, back to the misery of Quang Tri, in 1967.

On more than one occasion, as he remembered his buddies dying for nothing, he would duck into a bathroom or hurry outside so Beaulah wouldn't see him crying. Some days he would recover quickly, or he was able to play it off like everything was okay. But sometimes he couldn't ignore the memories and instead of crying, he just withdrew and barely spoke to anyone. He was still trapped in Nam, thirty plus years from the day he left. Beaulah could never understand, nor could he ever begin to explain. Besides, his experiences with his past wives proved that the women in his life could care less about what Nam did to him. Their main, and only, concern had been for themselves.

Curiously, Ralph saw no clear distinction between the women in his past and the nation as a whole when it came to vets like him. *B***hes! Just like the rest of America. They blame us for killing those they sent us to kill. We were marines, and we went where we were sent and killed who we were told to kill. Our country sent us. We did the best we could, and they thanked us by spitting on us when we returned home.* He wondered what people would think when they read his poem on that very subject. It was one that exactly reflected his feelings.

Spit

What if you went off to war
And no one gave a damn
To fight and die for nothing
Just like in Vietnam

To suffer the horror of battle
Never to be the same
And then have the folks back home
Regard you as the blame

Abandoned by a grateful government
Worth less than a Viet Cong pet
We're the vets of Vietnam
On whom you love to spit

But we would never spit on you
For wanting to end any war
That's why we just can't understand
What did you spit on us for?

Ralph raised the carbine and stepped back from the window. He put the weapon's scope to his eye and began to survey the streets below. The short woman with Beaulah's face moved around behind the scope's crosshairs. Ralph moved the scope from the woman's face to her legs. It had been Beaulah's legs that he had first noticed, and he liked that they were short and cola bottle perfect. Ralph frowned as he focused on the woman's legs in the scope; hers were frail and thin.

He missed Beaulah. For a second he toyed with the idea of shooting the woman across the street for having skinny legs. He was about to laugh when suddenly it came to him again how Beaulah would feel when she heard the news. She would be ashamed and maybe even blame herself; she was that kind of lady, always wishing everyone the best. She once referred to herself as a love, peace, sixties person. Her optimism had been something that Ralph had loved and even more, hated about her.

It was time. Ralph's hand shook, but only a little. He took a couple of deep breaths to rid his stomach of the butterflies that threatened to make him throw up. Then, for no reason, he lowered the carbine and just stood in the window with his whole body shaking. He tried to relax by thinking about Nam. Almost instantly, a combat mission ran thru his mind.

Chapter 4

The Marine

In his headset, Ralph heard his co-pilot, Captain Smith, yell out, "We're taking fire!"

"I see it," Major Hightower, the pilot, said calmly, and without warning he banked the heavily armed gunship (call sign Hostage 1) sharply and drove it at the shooting tree line.

Smith called out again, "Guns, guns, guns! We're already hot!" With six 60 mm machine guns firing, the gunship was aimed at the enemy and screamed to earth. Even while his own ship was making its gun run, Ralph saw the CH-46 helicopter (call sign Seaworthy) that they had come to provide cover for, attempting to land near an outnumbered and surrounded marine reconnaissance team. They were huddled in a bomb crater and fighting for their lives.

"Hostage 1, this is Seaworthy!" Ralph knew that Seaworthy's pilot was intentionally using his gunship's call sign to remind his crew that it was their job to protect him as he attempted to rescue the marines on the ground. "We're taking heavy fire! Say again, heavy fire!"

In a heartbeat, Ralph's gunship switched targets and began firing at the same enemy that had targeted Seaworthy. By some miracle, Seaworthy had finally reached the ground. From his vantage point, Ralph could see small trees falling as the Seaworthy door gunners opened up with their big 50 caliber machine guns. At the same time, Major Hightower had repositioned Hostage 1 and was also pouring gunfire into the enemy position below. Ralph saw so many tracer bullets flying that it was hard for him to imagine that there were four bullets, which could not be seen, flying in between each tracer.

The marine extraction was becoming even more intense. Enemy rounds busted through Hostage 1's cabin causing flaming sparks to shower Ralph and the other door gunner. The radios were filled with exited fear-filled voices. The ground RTO (radioman) began yelling at Seaworthy, "You're getting your butt shot off! Wave off—wave off!" All the while, Seaworthy was requesting Hostage 1 to direct him to the LZ. In a loud, take command voice, Major Hightower calmly told Seaworthy, "Take a heading of 180; drop and hug the tree tops. Seaworthy, the LZ is less than three (3) clicks at your 12 o'clock, be advised that we are at your 6 o'clock—with rockets and guns."

As the helicopters approached the landing zone, Ralph spotted several NVA (North Vietnamese Army) soldiers moving a heavy weapon in the direction of the LZ. He quickly turned his M-60 machine gun and had just started to fire at the enemy when the worst happened. "I'm hit! I'm hit!" The voice was loud and coming from the ICS (internal communication system) of Ralph's own gunship—not over the radios.

"Who's hit?" Hightower yelled it over the radio while at the same time banking the gunship hard right to evade Charlie's gunfire. Ralph and the door gunner were caught off guard and thrown about like rag dolls. It was only when Ralph grabbed onto the back of the co-pilot's seat to pull himself back up and while reaching for his machine gun, did he realize who was shot. It was his own co-pilot, Captain Smith, who had begun to jerk dangerously around in his seat.

Despite the helicopter bouncing about in the sky in its desperate attempt to avoid being hit, Ralph managed to pull the two red switches on the back of Captain Smith's seat. That allowed two large spring coils connected to the seat's back to pull the seat backwards and up. That removed the threat of the wounded officer hitting and kicking the chopper's duel flight controls as he trashed about in pain. Now it was easier for Major Hightower, the surviving pilot, to control the helicopter. Suddenly, sparks begin flying around inside the helicopter as metal gave way to Charlie's gunfire. Twice, Ralph instinctively ducked away from the large sparks of burning metal that showered him.

Looking up, Ralph saw two large, fist sized, holes by the storage compartment, which told him that they were under fire from heavy weapons. It took at least fifty caliber rounds to open up holes that big in his helicopter. The co-pilot was still screaming in pain, but there was no time for him now. Ralph knew that Smith was mortally wounded and that his screams would soon turn to silence. He scrambled to get to the open doorway and his machine gun. It was not easy to negotiate that foot or two as the pilot was jerking the helicopter all over the sky trying to avoid the rounds from the enemy's automatic weapons. Charlie was throwing everything he had at the helicopter, but Ralph made it. He pulled the M-60 forward and began firing into a tree line toward a glow caused by flashes from the many guns below. The glow looked like a line of lighted Christmas trees with flashing red and orange lights.

The first indication Ralph had that they were being shot down was the steady frog-like sound of the low rotor RPM horn. Major Hightower called it out, "We're going in, strap in back there. We're going in!" The helicopter was in a sixty degree bank and losing altitude fast. It was obvious to Ralph that the major was attempting to get as far away from the shooting tree line as possible. For now, it was a seemingly controlled crash to the ground.

Ralph took a quick look at the gunship's instrument panel. The transmission pressure light was on along with the master caution and several other lights. In his mind, it was over. He could only pray that they reached the ground before the gears in the transmission ground themselves to pieces; that was sure death. He realized that even if they survived the crash, they were deep in enemy-held territory. Rescue would be tough and Charlie would come out in force to finish them off. The "Rag Man," (another name the marines used to refer to the enemy) hated helicopter crews with a passion, and they were given a reward for bringing choppers down and killing the crew members. That reward was said to be thirty days R&R (rest and recuperation) in his home village and a new bike.

Shooting now was useless. Ralph let go of the machine gun. If they crashed now he would be torn in half by the large gunner's belt that he was required to wear whenever it was necessary to move about in the limited space of his gunship helicopter. It had happened on more than one crash; crewmen ripped apart by the gunner's belt while being thrown around in the helicopter. He reached for his seat belt. The ground was coming up fast to meet them now. Very fast! Ralph's last thought before the impact was about what his grandmother would think when she got the news of his death.

The Marine

Mama

Mama was against the war
Many times she told me so
Mama wanted me to stay
But mama I had to go

I talked of Core and duty
Mama cried and hung her head
Mama told me son be careful
And she said she was afraid

Mama suffered thru my first tour
Praying and writing every week
And when that tour was over
It was Mama I went to see

I could always talk to Mama
Our love just grew and grew
I never spoke to Mama of Vietnam
But I believe that Mama knew

My first lie to Mama
It was crazy what I felt
But I had to return to Vietnam
To try and find myself

Mama died disappointed
Such plans for her only son
Sleepless nights and flashbacks
Semper-Fi, I'm sorry Mom

Ralph slowly returned to the present. From below, the noises of an awakening city drifted through his open window. The noise reminded him that it was time. *It's best to start with the carbine*, he thought. That way, after the police barricade was set up, he could switch to the Remington 300—the weapon preferred by marine snipers in Nam. With the scope he was using, he could hit a target twice the distance that he figured was needed to reach any police snipers. They would certainly occupy the tall, seven stories building to his west at 7th and Spring Street. But there would be plenty of time to worry about police snipers. He figured to get at least two or more before they realized he had the Remington. Snipers were, in general, careless people because they (whether military and most certainly the cops) rarely got their asses shot off. Today they would be surprised.

Taking a marine-taught sniper's position to minimize the rifle's blast, which could be seen from the ground, Ralph figured that if it went the way he planned, most of the victims would be killed in the first few minutes of his attack. Everything was ready. He reached into his right jacket pocket and pressed the button on his Walkman, starting the tape. He then used the same hand to put on his earphones. Percy Sledge's voice was loud and impressive, drowning out the city's street sounds.

The words are so true, Ralph thought as he sang along with Percy: "And if she plays him for a fool, he's the last one to know..." He stopped singing and started to cry. As tears rolled into his mouth, at least the salty taste actually helped to ease the dryness. Crying had come so easy and often in the last few years, it had also become a real embarrassment. "But today," Ralph whispered to himself, "it don't mean nothing. I'm doing this." With the music of Percy Sledge still playing loudly in his head, he placed the stock of the carbine onto his shoulder and returned to the sniper's position.

The Marine

He relaxed as he looked through the weapon's scope onto the bustling downtown streets of Los Angeles. A man in a gray coat and baseball cap popped into its crosshairs. The man walked with a limp, seeming to favor his left foot. Ralph focused the crosshairs just forward of the man's ear. Suddenly the man turned allowing Ralph to look directly into his face—it was wide and in need of a shave. His eyes were large and seemed to bulge out. He reminded Ralph of an Indian he had seen in a Real West library book. The scope enlarged the face by a factor of several times with the black crosshairs of death resting on his forehead; almost exactly between the man's eyes.

Ralph thought, *No good. Better let him start walking again.* A straight hit in the face and the man would fall straight backwards and like an arrow, point to his window. Then, as if he had heard Ralph's thoughts, the man adjusted his cap, turned half around, and continued his walk down 7th Street. Ralph tracked the slow walking man for a step or two.

Suddenly, Percy stopped singing. Without pause, the Rolling Stones' sixties hit, "Satisfaction," blared out. The song instantly brought back the memory of the near riot at his last high school dance. An all-black band had dared to play that song, but managed to play it well enough to prevent the entire student body from reaching the stage and tearing their heads off. Ralph smiled at the memory and noticed that the man in the gray coat, with the baseball cap, had moved from the carbine's sight and in his place was a marine. *No!* Not just a marine, but one that looked like the same marine that he had seen earlier.

Oh crap! Ralph shook his head, took a step back from the window, and leaned forward just enough to see out without exposing himself. He observed the mystery marine who was also watching him—he was sure this time. Ralph relaxed his grip on the carbine and lowered it. There was something familiar about this marine. The way he stood and the way he wore that garrison cover with the black bill nearly covering his eyes. Still, it was only when Ralph saw the sergeant stripes that he remembered Sergeant Polaski; also known as Ski-Bo.

The marine across the street looked just like Ski-Bo, his old section leader during his first tour in Nam. *What a trip. But hell, Ski would be my age!* He certainly couldn't be that young buck he had in the cross hairs of the carbine. Ralph froze as he tried to make sense of what had just happened. *No! It couldn't be. There's no way! Ski-Bo? Hell no, Ski would be at least sixty four years old.* Ralph probably wouldn't know him if they were standing face to face. The marine he had seen wasn't more than twenty-something. Shaking his head he said aloud, "I better get a grip. I'm tripping."

Anyway, it didn't matter that it wasn't Ski; it was a leatherneck. "Dammit! Leave it to a Jarhead to screw something up!" Ralph heard himself say the words as he flipped the carbine's safety to safe.

He sat down with his back resting against the wall next to the window, and looked at his watch. *You got two minutes to get your ass out of this ambush, Jarhead!* "Two minutes!" He said it aloud, before reaching into his jacket pocket and removing the half-smoked joint. He was just about to light it when he jumped up and looked out the window again. The marine was gone.

Leaning with his back against the wall, Ralph allowed himself to slide down it until he was sitting on the floor. After a second, he lit the piece of joint with a shaking hand. He took a long heavy drag, held it, and released the smoke slowly. "Ooh, ooh, ooh, baby, baby," Smokey Robinson cried into his ears through the Walkman's earphone. "What the hell am I doing?" Ralph whispered into the cloud of smoke as it rose all around his head. He said it again, "Just what the f**k am I doing? Years of trying to do the right thing and it has all come to this!" He took another long drag on the joint and muttered the word, "Jerks," then couldn't remember why he even said it. *Thank God, the weed is working.*

He laughed aloud, happy that there was something he could always depend on. Weed was the only good personality he had. How lucky he had discovered it, in the Nam. Suddenly, he felt like he wasn't going to do it. *By now fool,* his watch said, *you could be dead already. Maybe you blew it! You're still alive, still in pain, still in Nam, and still failing in the world.*

He rested his head between his legs; arms wrapped tightly around them. His body rocked back and forth, slowly hitting the wall. The song, "Mercy, Mercy Me" by Marvin Gaye, came on the Walkman. "Oh mercy—mercy me—things aren't what they used to be." Ralph thought that Marvin got that right. As far as he was concerned, things would never be what they used to be, at least not before he went to war. For him, it was the war—always the war. He just listened and thought of one of his poems.

Al Sutton

Always

The war is with me always
No matter where I go
Why remember such pain
I guess I'll never know

Each day a different battle
All fresh and crystal clear
In Nam I prayed to go home
At home I live in fear

Putting faces on the dead
The enemy long since gone
The world moves on without me
I fight the past alone

The war is with me always
Terror within my mind
Where the dead remain alive
And sixty-nine remains the time

The Marine

For some reason, Ralph thought about the people that lived in his building. Most were former homeless and even today, hopeless. He hoped that all of them would get out safely. There were a few that he knew personally. The manager was an old woman, in her seventies, whose name he could never remember. She'd been nice to him and let him move in without all of the required deposit money. Her apartment was on the first floor. He hoped she would be able to get out long before the police arrived.

Now Mitch, on the other hand, was the one to worry about. Mitch was a bitter, mean, old fart who took great pleasure in arguing with Ralph. He insisted that WWII was a real war and that Vietnam wasn't about anything. At first, Ralph and Mitch didn't get along at all. In fact, he avoided Mitch for a while, and that was easy since Mitch had lost both legs in his big war. But strangely, after a few months, Ralph came to like Mitch. He complained a lot, but he also listened, and he never took crap off anybody. He often refused help, preferring to depend on himself, despite the wheelchair. For Mitch, his current home was just a place to wait on his social security check and death.

Bill was another neighbor that he had come to know. Bill had suffered a nervous breakdown while on the verge of becoming one of the youngest vice presidents of a multi-million dollar corporation. Ralph often felt sorry for him. He was a young man that could barely walk, barely talk, or do anything alone. Spit constantly ran out the side of his mouth. Ralph wasn't sure if Bill wouldn't be better off with the quick death a bullet would bring, rather than the years of slow death he was living. He just shook his head.

Why was he even thinking about them? There was nothing that he could do. His mouth twisted into a strange smile, as he thought about how the people in his building would brag that they knew the man who killed all of those people and then shot it out with the pigs. To them, he would be a hero, a real hero of the ghetto. Ralph could easily picture one of them telling America that, "You can only put a man through so much. Eventually, somebody on the good side of life, with everything to live for, has to pay for the way they treat the rest of us."

Ralph perked up as he began to ponder things that no one else seemed to really care about, but that he prided himself for understanding. One of his beliefs was that someday, everyday Americans would realize that if they ever expected jobs to return to America it would be necessary to kill every CEO who sent their jobs overseas and made huge profits on the backs of the poor and hopeless. They keep all the money to themselves—millions for them to live the high life. Meanwhile, normal fools like him were depending on their sell-out elected officials, like President Bush. But, Bush's primary goal was to make sure his rich friends paid no taxes.

He also believed that the founding fathers knew the importance of the right to bear arms. This ensures that sooner or later, the unemployed, the homeless, the hopeless, and the tens of millions of good Americans who are victims of the very industries that they have built, will wake up. When that happens, they will hold the CEOs, who sold their jobs to cheap labor markets overseas, responsible. Anyway, he wouldn't be around to see it.

Where was a Bill Clinton when the country really needed one? He had cared enough about Clinton to write a poem dedicated to him. He fished it out and began to read.

Bill

Look at old Bill
That's my man
Up on Capitol Hill
Fighting those pray-for-them Republicans

Trying to give more Americans
A shot at the dream
Even attempting to tax the rich
Imagine such a thing

Health care for all of us
Lord, now that's a task
Could be we've found ourselves
A president at last

Now don't get me wrong
Even I got mad
About a certain little bill (NAFTA)
Old Bill helped to pass

No, Bill's not perfect
Name someone who is
But he's trying to do right by America
And that's rare on Capitol Hill

Ralph's admiration for Clinton did little to diminish his deep mistrust and hatred of politicians in general and Republicans in particular. He pondered his frustration, thinking: *We the people are so used to getting screwed by our so called elected officials, that when a good man comes along we are so surprised that we end up letting those for the rich, aka Republicans, give him a hard time. Even the pride of America, the so called middle class, could care less about the poor. Funny thing is, thanks to those Republicans that they voted into the House of Representatives, the middle class will soon be joining us poor; just as soon as the Republicans finish wiping out every union, except of course the Teamsters. They know better than mess with them. As for the rest of us, it's all talk and then we forget.*

Much of his frustration had been neatly documented in the stack of poems that told the story of his life. One of those poems, "Alone" had been devoted specifically to the plight of the poor in America.

Alone

The poor stand alone; unnoticed
Beneath the pulpit of their world
Condemned to listen to political magicians
Preach of a promised land made of words

Today a change is coming
No one will be left behind
United together, you know we can do it
Vote for me, now is the time

Unmoved by old words
Still they cheered
This was all about nothing
Except a free beer

With promising smiles and handshakes
Before dark the politicians with their magic words are gone
While beneath the pulpit the poor remain
Trapped, unnoticed, and alone

Al Sutton

Chapter 5

Insanity

Ralph was startled by a loud knock on the door. The tape player was off, and he had gone to sleep. Without thinking, he grabbed the carbine and stood up against the wall near the window. *The cops wouldn't knock and besides, I've done nothing wrong.* Not that you had to anything wrong to go to jail in South Central. "The hell with it," he muttered to himself as he slid the carbine under the bed and walked over and opened the door. "Corporal Ralph Ram?" a marine standing in the door said.

"Just Ralph," he replied, staring intently at the young marine.

"You don't remember me?" The marine questioned. He seemed surprised that Ralph didn't know him.

Ralph said, "Hey Man! I've been out of the crouch for thirty years. Why the hell should I know you?" Ralph spat out the words, realizing that he was angry.

The marine reminded Ralph of himself those many years ago. He was squared away, shoes shined, uniform pressed to the T, shirt and pants aligned, and utility cover exactly two inches from the bridge of his nose.

"It's me man, Ski! Semper Fi! Once a marine, always a marine!" Without waiting to be asked, the young marine pushed passed Ralph into the small room.

"Ski," Ralph said it more to himself than to anyone else. He said it again, this time confused, "Ski?" One thing he was not confused about was that this was the same young Marine that had been in his gun sight; the one that had been looking up at him. "So what can I do for you sergeant? And by the way, I knew a good marine with the same name as yours. Like I said, just what the hell can I do for you?"

"Well that's close enough Ralph," Ski said, looking around the small room. "You act like you don't know me, but you do. Your ass wouldn't be here if it wasn't for me, or have you forgotten Operation Charlie Ridge?" Operation Charlie Ridge rang a bell. The clock instantly rolled back in Ralph's mind. He leaned against the wall staring at the marine.

When Ralph first reached Nam in 1966, the "Ski" that he knew, was already on his second tour. They didn't hit it off right away. Ski was tough, mean, and lean as they say in the Marine Corps. His face seemed chipped from stone with cold snake-like eyes that would turn into a twinkle only when he was shooting at the enemy, or getting drunk.

The problem between Ralph and Sergeant Ski actually started two weeks before Ralph got to Nam. Unfortunately, a Corporal Winters, Ski's best friend from his home town of Shreveport, Louisiana, had been shot down and killed while crewing a gunship (WB-16). Some marines that knew Ski said it had changed him. Prior to that, they said that he never took anything seriously; he always had a joke or a laugh to break the tension of combat. After his friend's death however, he had changed. He had become cold and was a pain in the ass to the crew chiefs in his gunship section by constantly double-checking their preparation for combat, especially the machine guns.

Some said it was the gunship's four main M-60 machine guns that failed to fire that cost the crew of WB-16 their lives. Ski seemed determined to never let it happen again to any marine in the four

Insanity

gunship section that he was responsible for. His over-bearing persistence dictated that everything be as near perfect as possible. Ralph was assigned to be a crew chief and as Corporal Winter's replacement, he took the full brunt of Ski's power. He constantly grilled all his crew chiefs, but especially Ralph, about emergency procedures, ship's weapons, and their responsibilities. He seemed to be everywhere at once. During Ralph's first month in Nam, he came to hate Ski more than the enemy.

To make matters worse, in Ralph's mind, Ski would often pull him off of an extremely dangerous mission and fly the mission himself. "You're not ready for this land of a crap sandwich, Rookie," was all he would say. Ski seemed to be thinking that if he could keep Ralph alive, it would somehow make up for the guilt he felt about his dead friend.

Things came to a head one day when Ski tried to pull Ralph off of his chopper during a hot re-arm and re-fuel, before returning quickly to a combat zone. A sister gunship had been shot down. The crew had survived, but was pinned down just a few feet from their destroyed helicopter and fighting for their lives.

"I'll take it Rookie," Ski said as he appeared out of nowhere carrying an M-79 grenade launcher. It was the same type of weapon that he had refused to let Ralph carry on his missions. When Ralph had asked for one, even though the other crew chiefs had them, Ski had refused. "You could blow yourself out of the air, Rookie," is all that he said.

This time though, Ralph refused Ski's order. "Damn you!" he yelled. "I was good enough to be out there when they were shot down. It could be me out there, and I'm going back for them, so just back the hell off!" Ski stood for a second; in shock. Until then, Ralph had never questioned his authority. A cold, angry look appeared on his face. Ralph thought for an instant that Ski was going to punch him, but Ski just shook his head.

As Ralph climbed back into the helicopter, Ski stepped forward and handed him the grenade launcher. He pulled the belts of rounds off his shoulder and dropped them onto the floor of the gunship next to Ralph's feet. "You might need these when you get back out there, marine." Ralph nodded, as the helicopter skids got light and the chopper began lifting off the ground. Despite a major effort to save them, all four crew members of the downed helicopter were killed.

That night, as Ralph sat alone atop a bunk with several cans of warm beer, Ski walked up and sat with him. For a long time neither spoke. Finally Ski said, "They were good marines. I heard that they gave those gooks hell before their position was overrun. They died fighting with honor, like marines. Sometimes no matter what you do, marines die. So many lives are lost for nothing." He had spat out the words. He said nothing more, then turned a beer up, finished it, and angrily threw the can onto another bunker.

"Like machine guns that didn't work," Ralph said. Ski turned with surprise and looked into Ralph's eyes.

"Yea," Ski said, "Like machine guns that didn't work." Both men were quiet for several minutes, and then Ski spoke again. "Marine, I know I've been hard on you, but I should have checked Corporal Winter's guns and because I didn't, a whole crew is dead. I promised myself after their deaths, that even if it costs me my own miserable life, I'm not losing another marine in my section due to dumb stuff. Dead without a reason is a great waste, Ralph. If I've learned anything in this place, it is that life is very precious and should never be wasted. Anyway, I'm sorry for being a hard ass." He extended his hand and after a hard handshake, stood up to go. "Just do me one favor will you?" he said, looking down into Ralph's face.

"Yea, Sergeant, what's that?" There was suspicion in Ralph's voice.

Insanity

"Marine, if you're lucky enough to get out of Nam alive, you need to make your life count for something. Live for those that won't get the chance—because of this stupid war."

Nodding his head, Ralph said, "Yea, sure Sergeant, that's a promise, but only if I live thru this hell of a war."

Ski smiled, threw him a salute, and jumped off the bunk. "See you at Zero Dark Thirty tomorrow, marine."

For the next six months, Ralph and Ski were buddies. In Nam, you wanted few friends—they died. But a real buddy was someone everybody needed. Ski didn't have a buddy, until he and Ralph resolved their differences. After Winter's death, Ski had seemed to only prefer working, flying, or drinking alone. Now, he had become human again through Ralph, even breaking into a smile or two. They both drank beer with the other men in their section and gradually, the whole section became close, including the normally distant pilots. And as a result, their squadron, VMO-6, became known for kicking ass. For two months, the section seemed to be charmed; they did not lose a single helicopter. That is, until Ski and the rest of his helicopter gunship crew was shot down.

On that mission, the pilot, Lieutenant Garbo, and the door gunner, Corporal Stones, had been killed in the first hail of enemy machine gun fire. They were dead even before the Huey gunship plunged tail down into the jungle. The co-pilot survived, but was badly injured in the crash. Ski, despite busted ribs suffered in the crash, still managed to pull the injured co-pilot, Lieutenant Peterson, from the mangled aircraft.

When Ralph heard that Ski's helicopter had gone in, he forced another crew chief, whose helicopter had been assigned to the rescue team, to let him go along on the rescue, as a door gunner. By the time their helicopter arrived at the scene, fixed wing aircraft and other gunship helicopters had beaten up the bad guys pretty good, but there had been no contact with the crew since just before they were shot down. Experience told them that 'no contact' was not a good sign and it had also taught them to be prepared for the worst. It was normal to assume that all crew members were dead. However, Ralph refused to even think normal. He volunteered to be lowered thru the trees onto the jungle floor to look for survivors.

Inside the mangled helicopter he found the broken, shot-up bodies of the pilot and the door gunner. He called Ski's name softly; aware that Charlie could still be in the area. After only twenty minutes of searching, Ralph was ordered to return to his pick-up point. Charlie had been spotted moving toward the downed chopper. Ralph was starting to panic but continued to search. He had to find his buddy, but it was actually Ski, lying beneath a clump of heavy bushes, that found him! Ski whispered to an astonished Ralph, "How about this! What the hell you doing down here, Rookie?" He then weakly pushed aside the bushes that also concealed a badly injured Lieutenant Peterson.

When they were safely on board the rescue chopper and headed to a naval aid-station (Charlie Med), Ski told Ralph, "I knew one of my boys would come."

"You kidding," Ralph said. "We flipped coins, and he, pointing to the other crew chief, lost. Just joking buddy, I was just lucky. Your whole gunship section wanted to stop the rest of the war and come get your ass."

Ski, nearly sleep from a shot of morphine replied, "That's real love, marine--that's real love. Hell, I'd come back from the dead for you boys. No bull! I will always be there for you guys, always." Then he blacked out as Ralph wiped the sweat from his forehead.

At a top speed of 120 knots, the huge helicopter got them to Charlie Med in about twenty minutes. When it was in sight, it seemed that Ski knew. He opened his eyes, looked at Ralph, and said, "Get the lieutenant off first." That was all he managed to say before he passed out again. Ralph thought, *that morphine must be some good stuff,* as they landed at Charlie Med and the medical guys came running toward the chopper. He continued wiping the sweat from Ski's forehead; glad that he didn't have to tell him that Lieutenant Peterson had died before they reached the medics.

As they took the Lieutenant's body off the helicopter, Ralph wondered how do you go home and live a normal life after this, or was this to be his new normal. He couldn't help but think, *this war crap is insanity.*

Al Sutton

Insanity

The truth is insanity
For a combat vet
Living with a pain
You can never forget

War means seeing yourself
As you actually were
When humanity was lost
And you were there

The cry of the wounded
The numbness of killing
The nightmare that
Came to be true

In Nam to survive
You embraced the insanity
But to live after the killing is over
WHAT WILL YOU DO?

Chapter 6

Destiny

Once Ski was past the door, he stood for a few seconds at the single window looking first one way, then the other. He turned around and sat on the window sill. "What's with you, Ralph?" He spoke softly, as if to a kid. Before Ralph could answer, Ski noticed the stock of the carbine sticking out from under the bed. He walked over to the bed and pulled the weapon out. Looking at Ralph, he removed the clip and the round in the chamber.

Ralph stared at him, suddenly angry, not because he unloaded the carbine, but for the question, "What's with you?" How many times had people asked that question over the past thirty years: friends, family, doctors, know-it-alls, and fools. He was about to say, "You wouldn't understand," but this was no ordinary person, this was Ski. This was the same Ski that had suffered through the steamy heat, the drowning rains, and the lost friends in Vietnam; likewise, the same as Ralph.

Ralph looked at the floor. *What's wrong?* There was something strange about this picture, but he just couldn't put his finger on it. When he looked up and into Ski's eyes, who was sitting in the window again, time stopped. As if relieved, he could say it at last, "I'm still there Ski, every day and every night. Everything I try sooner or later becomes

1969. Plus that, there's no help out there." He was pointing an angry finger toward the window.

Ralph went on, "The whole country is against us vets and has been since the end of that damn war in 1975. They just want us to fade away. We got a bum deal and now they're sending our sons and daughters over to fight in three Arab countries so Halliburton and their CEO buddies, can get government contracts. I say no draft and no war. You can't keep sending those young troops on tour, after tour, after tour, to a damn combat zone. Hell, I'm living proof of just what a couple, in fact, even one tour can do. It will blow your mind till they put your cold body in a cheap box and a government free plot. It's not right, but the average America could give a damn less as long as it's not them making the sacrifice." Ralph paused, then took in a deep breath; a little nervous about what he was about to say.

"Ski, I say this and hate myself for saying it, but 9/11 was, for a short while, a very happy day for me. The enemy had hit those Americans who didn't care about a soldier's sacrifice and look what happened. Our entire country shut down, and we didn't know what to do. President Bush sat in a kiddie classroom looking like a fool, instead of acting like a commander in chief. Yea, I was happy those assholes were so quick to send our kids to war." Suddenly, Ralph caught himself. He sensed that he was starting to sound foolish even though what he said was true. On that day (9/11) he glowed as the entire country suffered. It was like Vietnam had come to America—finally.

There was a strange, hard look on Ski's face that Ralph remembered from Nam, but the look in his eyes was not anger. For a minute not a word was spoken in the small room, and then Ski said, "You know how it is marine. If the country wants bodies, we give them bodies. If they had wanted to end Nam, we would have given them that too. We were simply marines doing our country's biding; nothing more, nothing less."

Destiny

"Yea," Ralph added, "bullet stoppers for civilians. I know you're right Ski-Bo," Ralph shook his head from side to side. "But the whole country treats us like dirt! As if we went there on our own and not by their orders. How many of us are surviving today Ski? Look how many gung-ho soldiers died during Nam. There were over 55,500 and even after Nam, veterans are killing themselves. Some of the best people this country had produced, put their asses on the line and now thirty years later, you got to walk on your hands and knees to get a little help from the VA. Not only that, people that burned their draft cards still hate us for going to Nam in the first place. Well, I'm not going to beg them to do what's right. I say death before dishonor, Ski."

Ralph's face was twisted in anger. He felt the tears coming, but he refused to let them run. The time for tears was over. "To hell with it," he said, more to himself than Ski. He opened the closet door and reached for the Ruger Mini M-14, for comfort. Ralph's voice was starting to break as he said, "The hell with it! It's all here Ski." He pointed to the ammo box. "The whole story and it's taken me two years to try and write it. My medals and my story are in that box. They will have to answer to me, because I'm going to kill as many of those self-centered assholes as I can before they get me." He raised a fist above his head in a sort of victory sign. "It ain't funny man—the crap just ain't funny. That's the bottom line." His poem of the same name summed it up even better.

Al Sutton

It Ain't Funny

It ain't funny at a party
When you're eating something grand
Then you think of what it would taste like
Cold, from a C-rat can

At first you kind of smile
Then you think of Vietnam
And your mind reflects awhile
Days of sadness, death, and bombs

In a room surrounded by people
You're feeling all alone
You attempt to push the memories away
But the damage is already done

That grand food wants to stick in your throat
And the party's no longer fun
Gooks in the wire!
FIRE MISSION! HELL PAPA 666411!

Destiny

For a minute, Ralph had almost forgotten that Ski was in the room. Now, he looked straight at him, shaking his head. "There's no other way Ski. I got a family, man, and I can't take care of them anymore. I've lost every job I've had in the last thirty years. I'm old now, Ski-Bo, still tripping, and I'm tired man. Thirty years in Vietnam is enough! Maybe, my kids can split the money from the story in the ammo can. I know that after today, some asshole will buy it. They will love it—anyway, something to watch the news for. It will be another crazy vet that went even crazier, you know. LIFE, TIME, CBS, NBC, ABC, CNN, MSNBC, and especially those Republicans at FOX will do hours of special reports about a vet killing innocent folks for attention. You know yourself that the news media loves what can't be explained. Who knows, my thirty seconds of fame may spark others out there just like me to…"

Ski interrupted again. "I see you've got it all planned, but listen to this. You were part of the best fighting force this country ever put into the field." Ski stood and walked around the room as he talked, moving like a drill instructor. "And we fought an enemy that has been fighting somebody on his own land for nearly a hundred years, non-stop. They were better than good soldiers. They were the best, and we kicked their asses! God rest their souls. We piled their bodies high outside our bunkers and left the jungles littered with pieces of what were once human beings. We called them Gooks, RPMS, Zipper Heads, Charlie, and Ragman. We left our own there too: Chops, Leroy, Buck, Mud Bone, and Chief. They were our friends—no—more than friends, our comrades."

Ski stopped pacing the room for a second and stared hard at Ralph, then continued. "You owe them Ralph. For every soldier that didn't return home, you must live your life as best you can, not like a fool or a loser. You can't say that VA hospitals are full of ambitious, non-caring doctors, or American women have no idea how war has affected their man." Ski placed his hand on Ralph's shoulder. "Ralph, the American people haven't experienced the horror of combat since the civil war, and you're right, our politicians are happy as hell that the American people choose to blame us, the fighters, rather than the promoters, themselves. And it's also true, marine, that many vets have died after the war; in fact, many were left alone with no one that could possibly understand them. They drank, drugged themselves, and some vets, too many, took their own lives. I agree with you marine," Ski said. "The country owes us, and you should tell them, but don't give them the satisfaction of saying, "I told you so," by dying. Piss them off, marine, by living! Show them how tall a marine can stand, despite a trip to hell and despite the fact that you're still in hell."

Ski stood over Ralph, looking him straight in the eye and said, "You should be happy that few Americans experienced what we did. Here's what you do, instead of doing something stupid, write that story. Tell America what they don't know about the war and the men that fought it. Bottom line marine, you can't blame the whole country for Leroy, Chops, Mud Bone, Chief, Buck, or the other 55,500 plus that gave their lives in Vietnam. Look, there are not many of us left now — combat vets from the old days."

"Hope those left are doing better than me," Ralph said; not feeling so alone for the first time in many years. Ski simply smiled.

"There's a new weapon in town," Ski said.

Ralph said, "And just what is that?"

"It's there," Ski said, pointing to the M-60 ammo can. "Right there in that ammo box."

Ralph replied, surprised, "How the hell do you know what's really in there?"

"I know lots of stuff," Ski said smiling. "You'll understand later, but what's more important is that you use it for good. People need to know about Nam and its after-effects on America's protectors and if there's more of these in that box..." He held up a couple of poems he had picked up off the floor.

"You read those?" Ralph asked.

"Sure did!" Ski said. "And I think they express well what many vets feel. Put them together as a book and use it, not just to help our own, but also the men and women fighting and coming home from the wars right now."

"You got to help me, Ski-Bo," Ralph said matter-of-factly. "Help me organize, man. I don't even know where to start. I've tried, but I'm pretty messed up. I can't stick with anything long." Ralph sensed he was punking out, but he didn't care. He didn't want to be alone anymore.

"Semper Fi, marine, I'm with you," said Ski as he took the small joint Ralph was about to put in his mouth and threw it out the window. Then he said, "Let's get busy. Show me something."

Ralph thought for a moment, then said, "Look at this. I wrote a poem based on the story of a brother that belonged to my old Vietnam Veterans of America, Ezell Ware Jr., Chapter 713, of South Central, Los Angeles. His name is Jack. He got shot up pretty bad in Nam and every day he requires a ton of morphine and other crap the VA issues to him to try and ease the pain. I called him my hero when Chapter 713 was still a chapter. Believe it or not, I was its president, until drugs took me down. Anyway, 'Destiny' is the title I gave to the poem."

Al Sutton

Destiny

I never thought of taking another's life
The army was about being all I could be
It was to be a temporary break from college and my love, football
Unaware it was of a killing field in the South China Sea

Paratroopers, the army's best, that was for me
The recruiter said basic training and I would be off to Germany
Jump school, jungle training, airborne, and then, straight past Europe
Onto the sea of my destiny

The war started with a cooking heat that you could see as well as feel
Leaving the plane I couldn't imagine anything worse
Than those hellish heat waves
Rising from the earth

My first day in Vietnam
While thinking what could be worse than this unimaginable heat
Some distance from the airfield I heard gunfire
And I start to imagine worse

Leaving the plane, incoming and outgoing soldiers pass
The unknowing and the aged young survivors
The survivors laughed at us
And asked for our girl's phone numbers

It would have been funny
Except there was no humor in their voices
They laughed without smiling
And no life appeared in their eyes

Destiny

Vietnam day three, night training patrol
We are ambushed and enemy bullets scream thru our unit
It's my first experience with organized madness
My butt tightens so much I couldn't pass a bb

Time stops on, I want to live
When time resumes
I see my first KIA (killed in action)
Our trainer, a second tour vet is dead

At my unit, I'm the FNG (f**k new guy) and it's screw the FNG week
As FNG I am assigned to carry a 'Prick 25' (radio)
To the Ragman
Radio men, like machine gunners are first to die

Vietnam for a grunt was frightening, but uncomplicated
It is unknown places, anytime battles, and enemy situations
Experience counts when engaging the enemy
But each experience is harder on the mind

The loss of brave comrades affects soldiers most profoundly
For me combat would void every human emotion
Except intense fear and loyalty to my unit
Death could come quick but only for the lucky

My friend, Lighting, was sick
He was holding his chest when we got the word
Reinforce a unit that's been pinned down by enemy fire
"Stay behind," I told him, but he refused

Al Sutton

We moved forward firing into enemy positions
Lighting was beside me...
BOOM (mortar round)
I wake up in a fog

Lighting has been hit, it looks bad, but he's alive
I try to care for him, "Medic," I yell
There are calls for a medic from everywhere
But the medic is dead

I hold Lighting
In my arms
He said he was hurting bad
Then he died

I'm a squad leader now
More than anything, I want to get my guys back home
I always take the point
As point man I'm good, or maybe just blessed

They are good, my squad
We get lots of kills and some captures
We are not gung ho, it's just that the higher the body count
The more they let us rest

Today the Gooks got Ellie, my RTO (radio telephone operator)
A homemade claymore mine
Filled with nails, screws, glass and Lord knows what
It didn't just kill him, it blew him to pieces

Destiny

I'm trying to get my men home
I'm trying to be a good soldier
I'm trying to lead my men, but I'm tired and this whole sick war sucks
God help us

About to go on R&R (rest and recuperation)
When my unit is ordered to Hill 875: the Monster
I could have sat it out, but my squad was going
Then so was I

It was supposed to be a
Simple cleanup operation,
Reinforce a sister unit
Under attack

As we started up, heavy fog and clouds covered the Monster: Hill 875
Like hungry wolves smelling a wounded prey
I could smell them
Only I was feeling more like the prey

Walking point, I'm the first to see our dead, it is surreal
U.S soldiers, they had been stripped of their clothes
Our brave comrades, shamefully naked
Their clothes and IDs torn up and thrown about

It's an ugly, evil sight
Made terrifying by the fact that their killers are still nearby
Near the top of the Monster, we find some survivors
They beg for water, food, and ammo

Al Sutton

Humping light, we did not have much to share
They told us horror stories
Including our Air Force accidently dropping a 500 lb. bomb
On their position

Eighty troops killed by friendly fire
A bad sign when those who care, kill us
Exhausted we hump on
Until the last of Third Company reaches the hill top

Within minutes, after the last soldier reached the top of the Monster
All hell broke loose
Small arms, automatic weapons fire, mortars, and rockets
Incoming!

Hardcore NVA had been waiting
Cutting us off...from reinforcements
For hours at a time, over a period of days
The fighting was horribly indescribable

On the morning of the third day
Helicopters under intense fire, with heavy losses
Got us ammo and supplies and got out the wounded
Though most had died

Our situation was desperate, defending was becoming impossible
An online assault was ordered
We had to overrun the NVA positions
Die trying, or just die

Destiny

One second I'm on the firing line, the next I'm thrown backwards
I'm hit. I'm down and in the open
Out of nowhere, a Private Louis drags me to cover
"Your leg," he yells

Louis was still firing at an NVA position
When suddenly, he was hit in the face
He grabbed at his face, and ran screaming into the open
I never saw him again

The bad guys were all over us
Then I heard screams
Someone yelled, "Bastards are killing our wounded"
Awful screams followed by gunshots

Wounded being killed
Unable to stand, I crawled under a pile of bodies
I laid there for what seemed forever
It was nasty: body fluids, feces, and blood from the dead all over me

An NVA soldier
Walked up to the pile of dead bodies and looked
God was with me,
He moved on past

A Sergeant Stone had joked that I'd need him one day
And it was Sergeant Stone that I heard calling my name
"Jack, Jack, Jack"
I screamed, "Over here"

Al Sutton

I was able to raise one hand
He pulled me from under the dead
With enemy fire popping all around us
The Sergeant carried me out of that killing field

And then it was over; a quiet and cries of the wounded
The battle ended
After a while, choppers managed to get in and I was treated
On the medical ship, Repose, I wondered how many survived

Destiny is defined as the seemly inevitable in combat
It seems that death is each soldier's destiny
And should a soldier survive his destiny
He will most surely suffer the pain of it the rest of his life!

"Damn, that's some mighty fine writing there Jarhead, how about hitting the old Ski-Bo with some more of that good stuff."

"Got one you'll love." Ralph said. He was happy that another combat vet was interested in his poems. "This is a poem that I wrote for my brother, Bob Sheppard. I call him my quiet hero. Hell, for over two years after I met him, I never knew he had been to Vietnam. He somehow got me to go to church, and it was only after I was over to his house after church, that I found out. Anyway, he was with the Twenty-fifth Infantry. When I saw the write-up based on his medal for action in Vietnam, I asked what Nam was like for him and asked if he would mind if I wrote a poem about what he told me."

Ralph went on to say, "Bob was a good man, a deacon and the best friend a man could have. When he died from Agent Orange, I damn near lost my mind. I miss him even now, years after his death."

The Twenty-Fifth

Second platoon is pinned down
Some hell hole near Cu-Chi
Charles got the high ground
Death feeds on the infantry

Life slows as the battle rages
Troops scramble as bullets zing
I empty a clip into a tree line
Soldier near me falls and screams

The rattle of gunfire is deafening
Charlie is walking his mortars in
The sergeant is going crazy
A headless body is his best friend

Confusion and panic engulf us
It's the worse we've ever seen
I forget that I'm a soldier
Staying alive is everything

Thru burning eyes I search the jungle
Enemy tracers reveal my sins
Ambush is what we've feared the most,
Lord, God please make it end

The Ragman's trap is closing,
"You die," yells a thousand VC
Then the crazy sergeant stands and screams
TWENTY-FIFTH INFANTRY!

Al Sutton

Insanity grips our unit,
Every sixteen on rock and roll
Second battalions attacking
The Twenty-fifth our battle call

Through hobo woods, like bolts of lightning
Thru death soldiers allowed to live
Hell's marriage
The devil and we are kin

It ends quickly, just like it started
Pitiful cries and dying moans
The guilty stare of dead men
And thoughts of going home

Chapter 7

Rehab

In the days that followed, Ski insisted that Ralph get into shape. Early every morning they would run, followed by push-ups and sit-ups. They would run to the park and work out Marine Corps style. It wasn't easy for Ralph though. Years of cigarettes, cocaine, alcohol, and weed had taken its toll on his sixty year old body. But slowly, after nearly a month of working out and writing at night with Ski by his side, life seemed to be worth living again.

They talked forever about the war; that is, the bad operations, the silly things that troops did, the lost buddies, and the many dead heroes. They never tired, often laughing and crying at the same time. For Ralph, it was an awakening. He told Ski about his relationships that had failed, or how he would just walk away from a job for any little reason. He also told of his time spent in jail ten years earlier. He had stopped paying taxes because he could never get help from anyone whenever he was down and out, and since Nam that had often been the case.

Ralph even confided in Ski about his girl, Beaulah, who had helped him and loved him despite his ever changing moods. The last time he saw her was about four months ago when, after an argument, he struck her across the mouth. He did it without thinking. "That's the truth!" Ralph said, still confused about the incident. He didn't even remember what the argument had been about.

"Sounds like you still love her," Ski said.

Ralph replied, "Yea, now I do, but I'm afraid for her. Until you came, all I could think about was feeling sorry for myself or shooting the neighborhood to pieces. Hey Ski, you think if we had been treated differently when we got home, it would have made a difference? Maybe we'd feel better about ourselves. Did you see the parades and the bull about the Gulf? Ralph rushed the words. "Did you see that man? I couldn't believe it! A four day ground war. HA! HA! A whole marine division sat on a ship as a decoy, and the VA is worried that these guys will have problems because they were expecting action and it didn't happen."

"No one remembers, Ski," Ralph rushed along. Charlie Ridge, Kha-Sha, Done-Ha, Operation Mead River, Hasting Two, and the Rock Pile." He took a deep breath and let it out slowly. *Now I'm doing what those fools in the nut house said do*. Surprisingly it helped. He continued in what was a more normal rate of speech. Ski simply sat saying nothing, letting Ralph's anger run its course. "Sorry Ski, guess I just got carried away."

Ralph looked ashamed, but Ski smiled and said, "Don't mean nothing marine, it don't mean nothing." It had been weeks since Ralph had an outburst like that. Ski stood and walked over to him, then extended his hand. Without thinking Ralph extended his. The hand shake ended with a hug and Ski said, "Man, you're an ex-combat marine. It's okay to feel. It's even okay to cry."

Tears came to Ralph's eyes, and then he responded to what Ski had said, "You were there too, but it doesn't seem to bother you!"

"Now don't start in on me, marine. I'm here to help, that's all. And just how is that book coming anyway?" Ski changed the subject and flopped onto the small bed. "Read me a few lines, Jarhead. And let the Ski-Bo know you got it together."

Ralph smiled and replied, "Ski, remember I told you how happy I was when 9/11 happened? Well, I kind of lied. I was some kind of pissed, even though I still believe that for our country, it was a wakeup call. Anyhow, right after 9/11, I wrote a poem called, "Too Soon." I knew it would be a long time before we would win that type of war."

"You got that right marine," said Ski. "Ten years so far and by the way, once a marine, always a marine, and no marine could be happy about what happened on 9/11. Now read how you really felt and make me proud. My time is getting short Corporal Ralph."

Al Sutton

Too Soon

Too soon the body bags
With the remains of America's finest
Will be returning home
To rest with earned honor

The soldiers will be buried next to hundreds
Of local heroes, firemen, and police
And the thousands of innocents
That perished on 9/11(victory will cost)

Too soon will
Our returning avenging soldiers
Their hearts pained by war
Still practicing how not to feel

Their minds refusing to rationalize
The horror of a war
That is destined to haunt them
Because of the death they somehow survived

Too soon my fellow Americans
The vision of war we see so clearly today
In our towering anger
Will become cloudy with our war losses

And our steadfast determination and resolve
Challenged each day by our fears
For not only are our soldiers
We are all this time in harm's way

Rehab

The war has come to our shores
Too soon as this deathly game of tit for tat becomes real
We will need God and one another as never before
For the enemy is hidden among us

If we are to survive this so called terror
Every America must find the hero
Within him and herself
Too soon, but not soon enough

The terrorist so willing to die for their cause
Will know we are
More than willing
And capable of killing them

Too soon
But no sooner than we share
With the entire world our freedom
Will we stand in righteous victory

And the enemy who
Seeks to impose his evil on mankind
Will be but a paragraph in the
History book of freedom

Too soon
Sadly as soon as the next generation
The heroes of this war
As with all wars will be forgotten

Al Sutton

As a new normal
Becomes the order of the day
And prayer our only hope of peace
Anytime soon

    Ski stood up and clapped his hands. "You publish your story and include those poems and you'll do our country proud. And our heroes can rest in peace, all of us."

Ralph said, "It's not all of that, but thanks for—in fact man—well thanks for everything."

Ski smiled, "The marines have landed and the situation is well in hand. You carry on Corporal Ralph Ramsey, USMC, and now if you don't mind I think I'll just get a little shut eye." He lay down on the pallet by the window as he had done for the last two months.

"Good night marine," said Ralph."

"You too marine," Ski said.

The following morning, Ralph woke up to find the pallet near the window empty. No Ski, but there was no panic. *Maybe he went to the store.* But curiously enough, now that he thought about it, he couldn't remember seeing Ski eat a thing in the two months he had been with him. He never ate; at least, Ralph had never seen him eat.

Suddenly, he realized the times in the park when, on more than one occasion, a few friends had spoken to Ralph during their workouts and not once did they ask who the guy in the jungle utilities was. *How could he stay away from his marine unit so long and how in the hell did he still look so young.* His final thoughts were on how silly he was thinking. *Ski was here, and without him I would more than likely be dead.*

Chapter 8

Autobiography of a Nobody

A gentle knock on his apartment door interrupted Ralph's thoughts. Ralph yelled from his bed, "Ski-Bo, you asshole!"

"It's Beaulah," a sweet voice that he had nearly forgotten answered.

Beaulah! Ralph paused before slowly moving toward the door. Opening it took a lifetime and when his eyes finally looked into hers, "Um, hi," was all he could say.

"Hi yourself," Beaulah said. She was as cute as ever, despite the serious look on her face. "John Thomas said he saw you running in the park last week, but it still took me the whole week to find you." She stepped into the room before he could ask her in. Her eyes moved over him from head to toe before she commented, "You look very good, Ralph! I was so happy when John said he saw you working out in the park."

"Yea, well," Ralph said. His heart was pounding! *God!* How he had missed her. "I've got a lot to tell you about. You won't believe it." Beaulah was surprised at Ralph's reaction to her finding him. She expected him to be angry or withdrawn. "Check it out, Honey," Ralph said out of the blue. "Ski, an old Nam buddy and I sort of got together after all these years. He's been the motivation for me these past few months." Ralph went serious, "Look Beaulah, I'm sorry about everything. I just thought you would be better off if I just got out of your life with all my problems and all. I loved you too much to keep taking you through..." Beaulah held her hand up like a stop sign.

She placed her finger to his lips and said, "No Ralph, I'm sorry. I didn't know how bad that Nam thing had affected you, Baby." She continued, "You never told me about it, but since the last time I saw you, I've talked to a lot of people, including your doctor at the VA. I've even been to a few meetings at the VA." She paused, and then continued, "Don't get any wrong ideas now, but it was for the wives of Vietnam vets. My friend, Jan—well, her husband is a Nam vet, and she said the meetings were really helping them. I won't admit to understanding everything, but I know now why you can't just put it behind you. I love you a lot, Honey." She lowered her head and closed the small distance between them.

Ralph could feel her body lightly touching his and her smell excited him. He wanted to hug, to squeeze, and to kiss her, all at the same time, but he remained frozen. Beaulah wasn't frozen however and took his face in her small hands and kissed him softly on the lips. His arms held her weakly as if maybe this was too good to be true. When their lips parted, he spoke very fast trying to keep her from stopping him again. "After I hit you, Beaulah, Honey, I knew you wouldn't want to be with me. How could you? How could you ever trust me not to do it again? But I knew. I couldn't take the chance that I might do it again." Ralph attempted a weak smile, but inside, his heart was pounding. He said, "Anyway, I thought that the only thing I could do to protect you, was to leave you."

"You love me that much Ralph?" Beaulah asked seriously.

"Yea," Ralph said, "I love you just that much." He lowered his head as he answered.

Beaulah cupped his chin in her small hands again and held his face to hers. "And I love you that much too, Ralph, enough to try and make this thing work. But, if you hit me again," she said loudly, making a small fist, "I'm going to make you pay! You know my mamma is from Louisiana and I got a little doll that looks just like you tucked safely away." Ralph laughed and Beaulah stared at him trying not to smile. Then she broke into laughter herself. When the laughing stopped, they came together, losing themselves in the passion of two people very much in love.

Afterwards, as they lay in each other's arms, Beaulah teased Ralph's ear with her tongue. She whispered to him, "Baby, don't you ever just walk away and leave me hanging like that. I wasn't worth a damn for weeks—I was so worried. You promise me right now," she said, then pulled gently on his ear lobe with her teeth. "Promise you'll give me a chance to talk you out of it."

"I promise!" Ralph said seriously, "I don't plan to ever leave you again."

He hesitated before continuing, just long enough for Beaulah to sense his unease, and say, "What is it?"

"We need to talk," Ralph said. "I need to talk," he corrected. They sat up in the tiny bed, side by side. Beaulah's eyes rested on the pallet near the window.

"You have a roommate?" She questioned.

"No—well—yes. My buddy, Ski, has been staying here the past few months. He saved me Beaulah. I'm too embarrassed to say from what, but without him, I don't know if I would even be around today."

"Where is he now?" Beaulah asked.

"I really don't know," Ralph replied. "He left before I got up this morning but I'm sure he'll be back. You'll like him," Ralph said happily. "We were in the war together. It's like the war had no effect on him at all," Ralph continued, shaking his head. Beaulah sat quietly holding Ralph's hand, surprised by how he was opening up to her. He had never talked this much about the war before. She wanted to meet this Ski and thank him. Ralph was like a different person, and so far so good; she didn't think she could love him any more than she did, but she did.

"Oh, Baby, remember the book that I was trying to write? Well, Ski and I worked on the book together and—wait—hold on." Ralph popped up like toast and went over to a small closet. Half opening the door, he was careful that Beaulah wouldn't see the rifles that were just inside; she was terribly afraid of guns. Reaching down, he pulled out the ammo can and sat it next to the bed.

"What is that Ralph?" Beaulah asked.

"This is an M-60 ammo can, Baby, but it's what's inside that I want you to see." Before he opened it, he looked deep into her eyes with a look of pride that she had never seen before. Ralph said, "Baby, you, of all people, can remember how long I've talked about and tried to write that book about the war."

Beaulah laughed. "I remember you wrote on everything in the house, except stationery."

Ralph laughed too. "That's the truth," he said. "But it never quite came together, until now." He didn't tell her he'd actually planned on someone else putting the book together after his death. "Close your eyes," Ralph said. Beaulah did as he asked. He opened the ammo can and pulled out the nearly completed book that was handwritten on school notebook paper. "Sugar, I want you to be the first person to read the 'Autobiography of a Nobody.' " Beaulah gently took the book into her hands and began to thumb through it. Ralph watched her as she read a paragraph or two then moved on to another page.

For several minutes she flipped pages, reading a few paragraphs from each. When she stopped, she hugged him, and whispered into his ear, "Ralph, it's beautiful."

He pulled happily away from her. "Thanks to Ski," he said. "Every night we talked and I would read a whole chapter to him. One night Ski said that I was kind of writing it for our brothers that didn't come back. And it was his idea to use all those poems that I've been writing about Nam since my first trip to the VA psychiatric ward in 89."

Beaulah's eyes lit up in excitement. "Oh my, I really want to meet this Ski. It's like he has given you a new lease on life. And the book, Baby, it's really very good."

"Beaulah," Ralph said in his excitement. "Tell you what, let's go find him. Maybe he's at the park working out, or something."

For nearly two hours, Beaulah and Ralph walked around the downtown area. They checked the local stores and then the park. When Ralph asked the park regulars if they had seen the man he had been working out with over the past many weeks, no one could remember seeing him working out with anyone; however, they did see Ralph working out alone. "Hell, Ralph, the only person I ever saw you with was you!" said Shorty, a wino and a regular at the park. Ralph was both confused and embarrassed. *What the hell is going on?* He turned to Beaulah and simply said, "After the liquor store opens, Shorty wouldn't see his own mother."

They walked in silence for several blocks toward Ralph's apartment. After the talk with Shorty, Beaulah had taken Ralph's hand. "Honey, we'll find Ski. Don't worry. In fact, I'm sure he'll be back. A man like that who has helped you to be what I see today, wouldn't leave you hanging." Then she removed her hand from his and placed her arm around his waist. "Anyway, I love what he has helped you to become." She smiled that smile that Ralph loved so much. "Maybe he's at the apartment by now," she continued.

"Hey, you know what," Ralph said, "I bet he is—I just bet he is." Just saying it made Ralph feel better, but God, he hoped Beaulah was right. Ski just had to be there. He wouldn't leave him hanging without a goodbye, or anything. In a sick way, it brought to his mind memories of how hard it was to say goodbye to marines who were going home from Nam and, even worse, it reminded him of Bill Clark, a former member of Vietnam Vets, Chapter 713.

After one of their regular monthly meeting, Bill had said, "See ya," like he always did. He then went home, and in front of his family, he sat on the front lawn and blew his brains out. Still feeling like he should have seen something was seriously wrong with Clark, Ralph had tears in his eyes. He had written a poem in his honor.

Forever Yesterday

Our chapter awoke this morning
To the memory of a friend
We realized without saying
We would never see Bill again

Despite the warming sun
Our cold won't go away
We are sad and a little angry too
You seemed fine yesterday

Talking and smiling yesterday
Life didn't seem so bad
There is shame because we were not there for you (Bill we didn't know)
You were all alone among those who cared

What, my brother, was on your mind
Could we possibly understand
What could be so very wrong
As to die by one's own hand

BILL CLARK, YOUR BROTHERS MISS YOU AND IN PARTING, WE CAN ONLY SAY, SEMPI-FI
WE LOVE YOU ......FOREVER YESTERDAY

Al Sutton

Chapter 9

News

After nearly two weeks of Beaulah's cleaning this and rearranging that, Ralph's apartment looked as if he had never lived there. Clothes in place, floor scrubbed to a dull shine, even the windows were clean inside and out. He was sure that without her, he would have slipped back to the days before Ski. Instead he waited to hear from Reader's Digest about his story that Beaulah had typed and edited. After she finished with it, Ralph would have felt proud to show it to James A. Michener, himself. But still, no word from Reader's Digest.

Ralph hadn't mentioned Ski much after the day they got back to find that he had not returned to the tiny apartment. At first, it was no big thing, but after two days he called hospitals to see if maybe he had an accident. From a pay phone, he even checked with the police. Ski had never mentioned where he was stationed; thus, his last hope was the marine bases at Pendleton and El Toro. Another little thing about Ski bothered him, also. Like how young he looked and even the old, outdated, type of jungle utilities that he wore. Only Beaulah's presence and the story they finished together had held his mind in check. He never told her of the inquiries he had made. Finally, for sanity's sake, he had forced it from his mind. This morning however, he was thinking how strange it had all been.

When the door lock clicked, he checked his watch—it was 08:20. He knew it was Beaulah. Since the first day after finding him, she had come to his apartment every morning after she got off work. "Hi Honey!" Beaulah said, as she entered the room. Her eyes were excited. She could never hide her happiness. Ralph thought, *Maybe she got that promotion she had been working on.* Beaulah practically dived on the bed.

"Why are you so happy this morning?" Ralph said.

"I love you Ralph, and I hope you won't be mad at me," she said, in one long running sentence.

"Never," said Ralph. Then he asked, "Why, what did you do?"

Beaulah answered, "Because I couldn't help but open your mail after I picked it up.

Ralph's whole body tensed. "Was it from…?"

But before he could finish, Beaulah screamed, "Yes, Yes, Yes!" She danced around the small apartment holding up the letter. "Yes, Yes, Yes, Yes, Baby! They're going to use it! Reader's Digest is going to print your story!"

Like kids, they hugged, danced, laughed, kissed, and even gave each other the high five. After a few minutes, Ralph sat back, read the letter from the Digest, and looked at the check. Chill bumps popped on his skin. Beaulah took his hands in hers and whispered, "You did it, Baby."

Ralph began to reflect on all he had been through; how the years after Vietnam had been full of torment to the point of planning his own self-destruction, as well as the pointless killing of his fellow citizens. But now, with Beaulah back in his life and—he looked at the check again—his life had changed. Now, anything was possible. And then he knew what he had to do: one final act that he believed would leave Vietnam in the past, where it belonged, and close the door on that chapter of his life.

Ralph stared at Beaulah for long seconds before he spoke again. "Honey," he said, wiping his eyes. "I need you to go to Washington, D.C. with me."

"What?" Beaulah looked shocked, "For what?"

"I don't know, just say you'll go," said Ralph.

"When?" Beaulah asked.

"Right now, just as soon as I can cash this check and get plane tickets," Ralph said.

"What about my job?" Beaulah asked.

"Please Honey," was all Ralph could say. "Please," he repeated slowly.

Beaulah could see it meant a lot to him. "Okay," she said. "But if I get fired, you are going to have to marry me."

"Deal Baby—you've got a deal!" Ralph said. Then he kissed her long and hard. *In fact*, he thought, *I'm going to marry you lady even if you don't get fired.* But there would be time to tell her.

He still couldn't exactly figure out what was going on with this Ski. A part of him prayed that nothing had happened to him, but for some reason a statement Ski had made way back in Nam keep coming into his mind. It was something about how he would come back from the dead if he had to for his marines. The mere idea that what he had been through in the last couple of months, actually didn't happen, was enough to blow one's mind. He still had to find Ski.

Later that night, lying in Beaulah's arms, he worried about the reason for his trip to D.C. He went to sleep thinking what a waste his two tours in Vietnam had been. *What a terrible waste*, was his last thought, before he fell asleep. He dreamed of the cockroach he killed in 1994, on a bad night, when Vietnam just wouldn't leave him alone. The cockroach paid the price of his misery. Days later, feeling very much like a fool, he had written a poem about it.

Al Sutton

Roach

Zero-Dark-Thirty, reality fading
Essential to find something to do
A cockroach aka Victor Charlie (Viet Cong)
Permission to kill, but not with a shoe

No, death must not come quickly
Charlie must suffer the fear I feel
Tonight a roach for therapy
My cure for now to kill

First I hit him softly
Just to slow his roach ass down
With a match I burn his antennas off
I laugh as the roach spins around

And around and around
When he stops spinning
I burn his ugly legs
Until they glow and smell

And when the roach was
Helpless and quivering
I welcomed him
Into my world

I kneel close until human and roach eyes meet
Important this roach should see
His death is not a natural one
It's being caused by me

NO! Don't die quickly roach
Please live as long as you can
Your fading life will be my strength
While my mind is trapped in Viet-Nam

Chapter 10

The Wall

The flight to Washington D.C. was a quiet one. Ralph spoke very little. It was as if he had climbed inside himself. Beaulah sensed he needed to be left alone and did little to disturb him. At the Washington Airport, Ralph hailed a cab. Once inside, he asked the driver if he knew where the Vietnam Memorial was. "Of course," replied the driver, "You a Nam vet?"

"Yea, I did a couple of tours," Ralph replied.

The driver said, as he pulled the cab away from the curb, "Heard it got little rough at times over there. I was in Korea, myself. I didn't see any action though."

"Welcome home—welcome home," Ralph said.

The driver responded, "Hey man—thanks. That's a first for me."

"Yea," said Ralph. "It took nearly two decades before it happened to me."

The ride, though it took only thirty minutes, seemed like hours to Ralph. No one spoke the entire trip. The clouds were dark and threatening rain in Washington; not unusual for the time of year. It was just the kind of weather Ralph loved. In Nam, heavy rain meant fewer combat missions. Some days they hadn't flown at all. He would always welcome the clouds that brought the rain and kept the little death dealing bugs called Huey Gunships on the ground. "God help the grunts," aircrews would say as they stood by waiting for breaks in the weather that would allow them to assist those poor ground marines still slugging it out with the Ragman; who always took advantage of the rain.

Ralph believed that between the rain and the politics it was a wonder that any American soldiers survived the ten years of Vietnam. In fact, as far as he was concerned, of the two, politics was responsible for killing most of the over 55,000 Americans that lost their lives. His mind raced back to the search and kill mission called Operation Hasting 2. That was the same operation where Ralph's gunship, Hostage 1, had been shot down and Captain Smith was killed. As a result, he and the surviving crew ended up trapped on the ground with marine grunts (ground troops).

The action took place just north of a hell hole called LZ Grasshopper, which was the last real combat base prior to entering the DMZ (demilitarized zone). American troops were barred from entering the zone. Just on the other side of the DMZ was North Vietnam, where the millions of Gooks, that hated marines, lived.

It was raining when Operation Hasting 2 started. The objective was to destroy several battalions of North Vietnamese Army soldiers massing to overrun LZ (landing zone) Grasshopper and its sister base, Dong-ha.

He had written a poem, which he called, "Open the Gates of Heaven," which captured the horror of that event.

Open the Gates of Heaven

As fresh troops
We first engaged the enemy less than two clicks from Dong-ha
We kicked their butts nearly
A click (kilometer) past the marine outpost LZ Grasshopper

In for less than two days of hard fighting
When the order came to stop the operation
Something about the border
Curving into the area where we were fighting (Politics)

We dug in until some heavies in Hawaii could figure it all out
We sat at our positions and watched the enemy regroup
Reinforce his troops
All within sight of our position

That rainy evening, with an increase in their numbers, they attacked us
We fought them off and counter attacked as trained
In fact we had pushed the enemy about another half click north
Then the order came to stop; something about the border again

We dug in again
We were less than five hundred yards from the DMZ
Now rumor control was saying that there was a
Five mile bubble in the border. What?

Meanwhile we didn't need field glasses to see the enemy regroup
Reinforce his troops again and attack
We, short of troops now
Had to retreat south 1 click

Al Sutton

After heavy fighting, we managed to form a second line of defense
We requested emergency troop replacement
About half of the troops requested were flown in
The order came for us to attack; retake the ground we had lost

The enemy resisted
And we paid a heavy price for every foot taken
After heavy fighting
We fought past the old position

The enemy was on the run
We surrounded and began wiping them out
When the order came to stop (Politics)
We had entered the damn border bubble (?)

This was getting very scary, exhausted on the edge of no man's land
We're too tired to dig in
Orders came from command
Not to fire on the enemy unless fired on by them (Politics)

Then we were ordered to retreat to some position out of the bubble
Retreat
We could see the enemy
Quickly regrouping with more troops than ever

Time was short
We had to try and dig in
Too late to retreat
Hurry dig in

The Wall

Long before we were prepared
With horns blowing and flags waving they attacked
The enemy hit us hard
Units were cut off from one another

Communications broke down
Everywhere, marines were being overrun
Panic, unorganized retreat happened
Leaving most of our wounded behind

Beyond exhaustion and disorganized
The enemy had only to press his advantage to wipe us out
But they stopped the attack
It got very quiet, and then we heard

The bastards were torturing, killing our wounded
Horrible cries, screams for help hung in the air
There was no order for a counter attack
But every able marine; even the walking wounded gathered together

Someone yelled, on line marines
We counter attacked (suicide)
We had to save our wounded
Or die trying

We met little resistance as we attacked forward
Sure, it was an ambush, but we kept attacking anyway
Until we reached the chopped up remains; our wounded
We were too late; just too damned late

Al Sutton

We could feel the enemy watching us
Guiltily gathering the mutilated body parts
Our fellow marines and comrades
Most of us cried, but no one said a prayer for them

Frustrated, beyond tired, sick with anger, guilt, and fear
We rushed in slow motion
Digging in next to the covered bodies of our fellow marines
We watched, helpless

The enemy regrouped
Brought up fresh reinforcements
And begin their attack; the marine next to me said
Open up the gates of Heaven Lord, here we come

Something crazy happened, we didn't care anymore
The fighting was insane, even hand to hand
Seeking revenge and determined not to leave our wounded again
We screamed the names of our dead

Attacking instead of defending; no retreat, no retreat, marines yelled
Despite their fresh troops and superior numbers
We butchered a surprised enemy
Deeper into the DMZ or North Vietnam; we didn't know or care

The order came to stop our attack, but we continued
A marine officer attempting to obey the stop order
Was killed by his own men
The killing of that officer stopped our unplanned attack

The Wall

It caused a split in our ranks
While we argued about
Whether those who killed that stupid officer
Should be reported or not

Our enemy regrouped
Amassed more troops than ever and attacked
We tried to defend ourselves, but the enemy was all over us
An everyman for himself retreat was ordered

But no one listened, we just fought harder
Better we all die, than leave even one marine behind
The enemy threatened to overrun us
But mad men rushed to fill the holes

It cost most of them their lives
Men on both sides fought, screamed, and died
It was hell on earth and then it was over
The enemy retreated; leaving hundreds of dead

For us it was no victory
Several marine units had been wiped out
Command decided to replace us with fresh troops
Just outside the bubble (Politics)

The fresh marines arrived the next day
Most were inexperienced
As we survivors got on the helicopters
We refused to look the FNGs in the face; they were dead men

Al Sutton

As I flew out
Praying never to return
I looked down from the chopper
On the ground

Safe on his side of the border bubble
The enemy seemed to be laughing
As they regrouped, brought up fresh troops
And prepared to attack

"Honey," Beaulah said, bringing Ralph back to the present.

"Yes Babe, what is it?" Ralph asked.

"Look over there. Isn't that where that Vietnam Wall begins?" Beaulah asked, pointing out the window of the cab.

"That's it alright," the cab driver answered Beaulah.

"Sure looks just like a picture I saw of it once," said Ralph. He hoped his voiced sounded okay. Actually, there was a lump in his throat the size of a golf ball. What he hoped was to prove himself wrong. What he had been thinking was way out of line and this would prove just how far.

Even before they got out of the cab, Beaulah could feel Ralph's body shaking a little. She had not even guessed that this was where he was taking her. She squeezed his hand. He smiled at her as he paid the cabby.

Just looking at that wall of fallen soldiers made Ralph weak in the legs and he leaned on Beaulah a little. He walked into the Memorial Office where a soldier at the counter asked him, "Yes Sir, can I help you?"

"Yes sir," said Ralph. "Would you see if you have a Sergeant Paul J. Polaski?" It took less than a minute on the computer to find Polaski's name.

The Wall

"Yes sir—Section A, Panel Ten. Want me to write it down for you, sir?" the soldier asked.

"No thank you." It was Beaulah who spoke, "We'll find it."

Ralph's chest was swelling and he felt a little dizzy, but still managed to let Beaulah lead him outside. As they walked past the wall, Ralph noticed a few other vets. Most were standing quietly staring at the wall. A few had their girlfriends or wives standing close or holding onto them. For some special reason, Ralph's attention was drawn to a guy who was standing alone. His hair was silver, long, uncombed, and protruding wildly from underneath an old jungle bush hat. Dark glasses covered his eyes. Ralph noticed the man's hand pressing a name from the wall onto the special paper provided for that purpose. Then he noticed the combat aircrew wings on his bush hat. That really got his attention. Ralph had been awarded those exact same combat wings during his first tour.

As they walked past the man, tears began to run down Ralph's face. Without warning, thoughts of Lieutenant Galbreath, a pilot he had flown many a combat mission with, came to his mind. He smiled; thinking of the time a new door gunner, flying his first ever combat mission, had asked Galbreath what was the procedure in case Galbreath was shot. For nearly two minutes, not a word was spoken by the lieutenant, the copilot, or the other crew members. They all knew better than to say a word in answer to what in Vietnam was a very stupid question. It was believed to be bad luck to discuss such things. Finally after a few minutes of silence, Galbreath spoke to the rookie door gunner. "What's your name?"

"Lance Corporal Williams," the door gunner replied through the helicopter's ICS (internal communications system).

"Well, Lance Corporal Williams," continued the lieutenant, "If I get hit and I'm killed, I really don't give a damn what you do—okay."

"Yes sir," replied the embarrassed door gunner.

Ralph had rubbed Lieutenant Galbreath's name off the Moving Vietnam Wall when it was in Long Beach, around the year 2000. The Marine Core promoted (posthumously) him to captain after he and the other three members of his gunship crew were killed trying to save a recon team.

Although Ralph left Vietnam almost exactly one month before Galbreath was killed, he didn't know, until that very year at the Moving Wall, that he didn't make it. He learned of his death after a conversation with a fellow ex-marine who happened to have a book with a list of all the helicopter crewmen that had been killed in Vietnam. He was shocked when he looked up the records for VMO-6 (marine helicopter fighter squadron) and found Galbreath's name. That's when he went to the computer that was provided to look up the dead and their location on the wall. He still remembered Galbreath's panel: 39 East, Wall Line 59.

A small gust of wind blew and a few drops of rain touched their faces. It took nearly twenty minutes to find the correct section of the wall. When they did, Beaulah kissed Ralph softly on the cheek. "Go ahead, Baby, I'll wait here," she said. Ralph didn't answer her, he couldn't. He just walked over to where the wall flowers were sold. A female voice said, "Only a dollar." He took a bundle of flowers, giving the girl a five dollar bill. Shaking his head, he told her, "Keep the change."

At the wall, he looked at the names one at a time in the A-Section, until finally, he saw PAUL J. POLASKI. It was as if the whole world suddenly fell on his shoulders. He touched the name. "Damn, Ski-Bo!" Ralph cried out the name as his legs left him, and he slid to his knees still touching the wall. Time stopped, and he wept as if he had never cried in his life. When Beaulah's hand touched his arm, he grabbed it and held it against his face. Without looking up, he simply said, "Baby, do you believe in God?" Beaulah just pushed her hand playfully, but hard against Ralph's head.

Ralph was quiet for a minute then he said simply, "I remember one day in Vietnam when Ski said something about taking care of us, the marines in his section even if, and I am not joking, I have to come back. I never assumed he meant back—from there." Looking back up, he said, in disbelief, "Right here—killed in action—right here," pointing a finger at Ski's name and date of death: Dec 1970. Ralph took a deep breath and said to Beaulah, "I know this whole thing must sound crazy, but Baby if you believe in a Loving God, I ask you to please believe me. He came back and saved me."

"It sounds like he just kept his word." Beaulah said. She went on to say, "I wasn't there Baby, but I know in my heart and by just looking at you, that Ski, thank God, just kept his word."

Ralph leaned the flowers against the wall under Ski's name and stood up slowly. "Sergeant Paul J. Polaski," he said. Then he gently pulled his right hand away from Beaulah, raised it slowly, and saluted. As he finished his salute, he said, "You did good Sergeant Polaski, you did damn good." Beaulah, crying herself now, said nothing. She simply put her arm around his waist and rested her head on his shoulder.

As they turned and begin walking away, it was Beaulah who spoke first, "Think he'll be back?" She whispered it into Ralph's ear. It was her way of letting him know that she believed him.

"I'm sure he will," Ralph answered. Then he stopped and swung around to look back at the Wall one last time. Turning to leave, he hugged his lady around the neck. "Yea, I'm pretty sure he will, as long as there are marines that need his help. Sergeant Ski... he'll be around!"

Al Sutton

The Experience

How many have stood before this Wall
With memories of those who gave their all
Today it was an old marine I went to see
And what an effect it had on me

A million thoughts of war
All rolled into one
As I saluted these men
And the deeds they had done

In the Wall I see their faces, smiling
Tranquil and forever young
I felt guilty for the decades of life they missed
And for every day I ever had fun

Not until I touched this Wall, of fallen comrades
Did I realize I was not alone
I left smiling; as I cried; like me, this Wall of Honor
Has brought them home

The beginning

Appendix A

The Nut Ward

MENTAL HEALTH
Author's actual notes from the "Nut Ward"
206D Westwood VA Hospital
Westwood, California

The names and events are from actual notes taken between the dates of December 17—December 31, 1996. After December 31, I was transferred from 206D to the PTSD Unit and remained there for the next 8-9 months trying to forget Vietnam—by being forced to remember.

Al Sutton, USMC
Gunship Crew Chief/Door Gunner
Vietnam: December 1966—January 1968
October 1968—November 1969

Al Sutton

Daily Notes
Tuesday, 12-17-96

1. Informed by Cynthia (my social worker) that I would be going to PRRP (Post-Traumatic Stress Residential Rehabilitation Program).
2. Pass to PRRP Party at 6:00.
3. Called and thanked Marty for call to Sever B. to get me into PRRP.
4. It's a shame other vets (including my friend John H.) must go thru so much crap. John really needs a PTSD tune-up. John's situation is exactly the same as mine. They (Cynthia) insist he has alcohol problem and insists he goes to RTC for rehab.
5. John raised hell with Cynthia at 12:00.
6. Good News, John going to PRRP Group Tuesday and Thursdays -- same as myself. Went to P.R.R.P. Christmas party. John told that only first timers to PRRP will be accepted; told so by P.R.R.P. director.
7. Jim D. told me would arrange for my screening to PRRP.

Daily Notes
Wednesday, 12-18-96

1. I talked to Jim D. about PRRP; should transfer Dec 30.
2. Note, without the help of Steve B., I don't believe it would have happened. Dr. G. and Cynthia insist I'm a damn alcoholic.
3. George V. very sick again and is unable to do anything for himself. Staff is aware of his condition. I'm scared for the man.
4. Birdie (staff) really trying hard to help him, God knows he needs to be in hospital, a real damn hospital. George V. said that Dr. G. gave him new meds.
5. Rick C. angry about his treatment checks out of this nuthouse.

6. PTSD Meeting: Dr. P. – side pool PTSD, Cynthia – Social Worker 206D, Dr. G. – Doctor Ward PRRP, Jim D. – Director of PRRP, and Staff- Birdie, John, Debbie (Good People).
7. Screening with Jim D. at 1:45 PM; screening went well, refused to accept anything other than PRRP because of 100% pay. Jim informed me of rules and discussed where I would live.
8. Dec 30 is when I should transfer to PRRP.
9. George V. is sick again. They took him to Building 500.
10. Ward 206D Christmas party.
11. John took 7 people on a long walk.
12. Rick C. checks out angry, goes to live at mother's house .

Daily Notes
Thursday, 12-19-96

1. George V. finally taken to hospital again; Zero Dark Thirty this morning. Birdie (staff) is to be commended for her caring efforts with George.
2. Continued screening with Jim D. and Ray (his assistant). Scheduled to go to P.R.R.P. Dec 30, 1996.
3. Johanna H. and I attended Vietnam Veterans PA meeting, Building 217 6-8pm.
4. Head nurse Rosemary showed little concern for George V. and in fact never left office to check on him. It was necessary for Birdie to go over her head to get help for the man, poor George.

Al Sutton

Daily Notes
Friday, 12-20-96

1. John H. is in a bad state of mind. Dr. G. and Miss Black want to send him to Haven. No PTSD help for John...jerks! John's talking crazy about hurting Dr. G. I'm worried.
2. John H. gets informed by Dr. G. that because of possible cancerous black thing on the back of his left shoulder, he will remain on 206D despite the other Dr. G.
3. Gill L. finally gets level 3; should have gotten after week #1 since he was not an alcohol or drug addict. Blame Dr. Asshole G.
4. I went to P.R.R.P. screening by PRRP community Vets.
5. John H. went to VA Public Relations; talked to Richard T., about staying on Ward 206D. Richard said he would talk to Cynthia. Black social worker does not expect any change. Reason: beds in 206D cost $500.00 a day; beds at Haven cost $200.00 a day. John's talking about suicide again.
6. Ward is under staffed; only three staff people on every shift.

Daily Notes
Saturday, 12-21-96

1. Uneventful
2. I took Clonazepam trying to sleep without nightmares.
3. A Jewish WWII Vet checked into Ward; Mr. S.
4. Ward is really full of people.

The Nut Ward

Daily Notes
Sunday, 12-22-96

1. I am concerned about three staff persons; all females; 18 males on deck. I guess 3 women can handle it unless there is trouble; then someone might get hurt. This condition is not uncommon on ward 206D.
2. Ward is nearly full of patients.
3. Staff is short of people due to holidays.
4. Margret, the R.N., is doing a double shift.
5. Will take Clonazepam to sleep; hoping to have no nightmares.
6. Mr. S. wants out; he is giving staff a hard time. I believe it was his daughter who had him committed. Staff refused to let him AMA (against medical advice) out and has reduced his phone privileges because he is calling different organizations to help get him out of here. I feel sorry for him.

Daily Notes
Monday, 12-23-96

1. John H. came here to Ward 206D on Wed 12-18. Claims to be an alcoholic and suicidal. Was a marine in Vietnam 1965-66 at Da Nang. Does not appear to be an alcoholic. He is in good physical shape; claims to have worked for Douglas on YAH64. I have reason to believe he is not what he appears. My brother, Holden feels the same. Must watch what we say around him until more information about him can be verified.
2. Robert T. and John returned today, (same day) both had slipped away when they got some money.
3. Margret- Double shift Sat/Sun, returned to work today, nurse appeared very tired.

Al Sutton

Code 1227-58-82191: Between 12-2, patient kills self on lot near post office (gunshot). Rumor—patient was not allowed to enter hospital for depression

Daily Notes
Wednesday, 12-25-96

1. Spent Christmas with family.
2. Returned at approximately 8:00 PM; had till nine but can't trust anyone.
3. Milton boy in wheelchair went on pass; returned dirty; interested to see what happens.
4. Pissed myself (urine test), thank God I'm clean.

Daily Notes
Thursday, 12-26-96

1. Mr. V. returned today to ward 206D, he looks well. Said he was going to ask for another doctor, would never let Dr. G. see him again.
2. Went to PTSD Group with Holden, Building 217. Leslie M. (a social worker) ran group. Entire 2 hours was worthless; talked about the hospital downsizing and taking care of yourself.
3. Dr. H. will have his 21 days in tomorrow. I'm happy for him; Dr. G. tried to get him out before his 21st day. Hospital and government working together.
4. Mr. W. (a brother) is being kicked out of the hospital; told to go to AA meeting. He was unable to go to Haven because of the medication he is on. He was only 6 weeks clean so he could not get into PTSD program.

Daily Notes
Friday, 12-27-96

1. Abe C. (veteran's benefits counselor) processed my 21 day statement so I might be able to get paid my 1005 within weeks after PRRP Completion. Office is in Building 500, across from canteen.
2. Checked on appointment for eye exam; confirmed date: Jan 27, 1997.
3. Called lawyers recommended by Morty; will drop state lawyer, D. They claimed they dropped me, for the second time.
4. Community meeting (I chaired, as president). Major issues: smoke breaks and staff not adhering to their schedules.

Daily Notes
Saturday, 12-28-96

1. Mr. S. attempted to run after no one was available to take him to the Jewish church of his choice.
2. *Note* Female staff without male staff has problems; lots of name calling, main word is, b**ch.
3. Saw Mr. W. at chow hall, they gave him another week; said they would try to find him a program and advised him to talk to PATZ to get on the list for PTSD treatment after 90 days of sobriety.
4. Smelled weed smoke on ward. Bruce (wheelchair) is the man. This is the second time. Staff seems to be aware of who it is, but no action taken.
5. Some patients complaining, but not to staff about weed smoke, while other patients are worried about taking down patients who said weed smoke jeopardizes sobriety. I can't understand it.

Al Sutton

Daily Notes
Sunday, 12-29-96

1. This is my last day on Ward 206D.
2. Wrote letter addressed to Nurse T. or To Whom It May Concern, about Bruce B. smoking weed on ward, several times. Nurse M. called the police but they said they could not do anything.
3. People involved in above action: myself (Al Sutton), Steven D. (Who asked to be removed from Mr. B's. room), John H., staff: Birdie and Nurse M.
4. Staff said Dr. G. is kissing Mr. B's. mother's butt; keeping Mr. B. on his ward for nearly six months because he received stuff for his computer (home) from Mr. B's. mom.

Daily Notes
Monday, 12-30-96

1. Transferring to Building 212, Room 340, bed 4; PRRP.
2. Felt sad leaving 206D. Will miss the staff people like Debbie, Birdie and my John H. who I plan to stay in touch with.
3. While packing, I was told of near fight between B. and Steve (the man who changed rooms because of B. smoking weed). The police came and took B. because of various reasons and then returned him right back to Ward 206d? Dr. G.!

Daily Notes
Tuesday, 12-31-96 New Year's Eve

1. Took VERY complete physical (Dr. R.).
2. Was told by Dr. R. of two vertebrae in neck that are losing the stuff that separates vertebrae.

3. Was informed of possible infection in lower lungs; will test for T.B. and whatever. Will take another chest x-ray in about a month to note progress of infection.
4. Was told cholesterol was twice as high as it should be. Considering medication. Diet important!
5. Funny thing, I don't seem to give a damn.
6. Went to group. Jim W. and Leslie were there. The subject of the hour: ways of choosing life over death. Regarding vet who shot himself to death, wondered why no news or newspapers covered anything about him.
7. Those non-caring jerks, killing them would have been a better choice, at least then one could make the 6 o'clock news.
8. Happy New Year; I'm alone.

On this day, a veteran of the Gulf War pulled a gun in Dr. B.'s office. She managed to run out of her office into a break room, where we were having a group meeting, yelling, "Gun! He has a gun!" The next thing we heard was the sound of a single gunshot. Once the gunshot went off, the remaining staff panicked and began to run from the building while we, the vets, ran toward Dr. B.'s office.

When we reached her office, the door was locked, so we did not think twice and joined forces to break down the door. When we entered the room we realized that this vet had shot himself in the chest. I bent down and grabbed his shirt to soak up some blood and to put it over the bullet entry. Another vet elevated his leg. Long story short, approximately five minutes passed before anyone came to help. The vet survived.

Also from Anointed Life Publishing:

DISCOVERING YOUR ANOINTING NUMBERS
By Carolyn Chambers

In her life-changing new book, Carolyn Chambers helps readers discover their anointing numbers and empowers them to fight life's great battle-themselves. Simply put—everyone is at war with themselves. But, walking anointed is something everyone can achieve. In, *"Discovering Your Anointing Numbers: Allow me to introduce You to Yourself,"* Carolyn Chambers examines the influence that birth demographics have on human behavior. This is a compelling read for all.

THE ANOINTED LIFE – CRUCIFYING THE FLESH
By Carolyn Chambers

Thoughts received from the flesh alienate us from the grace of God; while those received from the spirit bring righteousness, peace, and joy. The flesh cunningly attacks the will, the mind, and the emotions; keeping us in a state of immaturity and alienated from our inheritance through fear, doubt, and unbelief. However, thoughts received from the spirit position us to live the anointed life—a life lived under the influence of the Holy Spirit.

We invite you to visit our website at:
Anointed Life Publishing

www.anointedlifepublishing.com

www.ingramcontent.com/pod-product-compliance
Lightning Source LLC
Chambersburg PA
CBHW031423290426
44110CB00011B/506